Library of
Davidson College

Inflation Is a Social Malady

by Carl E. Beigie

with an appendix by Gennifer Sussman

BRITISH-NORTH AMERICAN COMMITTEE

Sponsored by
British-North American Research Association (U.K.)
National Planning Association (U.S.A.)
C. D. Howe Research Institute (Canada)

©British-North American Committee 1979
Short quotations with appropriate credit permissible

Legal deposit — 1st Quarter 1979
Quebec National Library

ISBN 0-902594-34-6
Library of Congress Catalog Card Number 78-70536

Published by the British-North American Committee
Printed and bound in Canada

March, 1979

To
Nick Campbell,

a member of the British-North American Committee until his death in July, 1978. He was a man of quiet dignity and compassion who gave generously of his time to help others. His ability to inspire will be deeply missed by those of us who worked with him.

Contents

The British-North American Committee .... inside front cover

Statement by the British-North American Committee
to Accompany the Report vii

Members of the Committee Signing the Statement viii

Acknowledgments xi

INFLATION IS A SOCIAL MALADY by Carl E. Beigie, with an appendix by Gennifer Sussman

I. **The Search for Discipline** 1
   Characteristics of Contemporary Economic Policy 2
   An Uneasy Compromise 4
   Summary of Contents 6

II. **An Overview of the Global Economic Condition** 8
    High Expectations, Disappointing Performance 8
    Basic Economic Performance Targets 8
    Falling behind the Targets 10
    Basic Causes of Economic Distress 11
    A Framework for Policy Analysis 18

    Technical Note to Chapter II 20

III. **Gradualism As a Policy for Restoring Equilibrium** 24
     Recognition of the Inevitable Comes Slowly 24
     Gradualism versus "Fine Tuning" 26
     Monetary-Policy Mechanics 27
     Fiscal-Policy Uncertainties 29
     Conclusion 33

IV. **Structural Problems and Their Impacts** 34
    Adjustment Rigidities 34
    Investment Constraints 36
    Efficiency Handicaps 39

V.	**The Role of Government: Intervention and Disincentives**	43
	Growth in the Size of Government	43
	Direct Impact of Government Sector Growth on the Inflation Process	46
	Contributions to the Inflation-Unemployment Problem	47
	A Concluding Observation	48
VI.	**Pragmatic Policy Responses**	50
	Designing a Strategy: Clear Lessons from the Recent Past	50
	Gradualism and Its Alternatives	52
	The Importance of Reason	56

Appendix: A Summary and Critique of the McCracken Report 60

Footnotes to the Statement 73

Members of the British-North American Committee 75

Sponsoring Organizations 80

Publications of the British-North American Committee ... inside back cover

Charts

1. Inflation and Unused Capacity, Seven Major OECD Countries, 1961-76 64
2. The Narrow Path Back toward Full Employment and Price Stability 66

Figure

1. A Model of the Inflation-Unemployment Process 21

Table

1. "Discomfort Index," Seven Major Countries, 1959-76 63

Statement of the British-North American Committee to Accompany the Report

The British-North American Committee has been concerned for some time with a number of problems in Canada, the United States, and the United Kingdom related to the slow recovery from the 1973-74 economic recession. But until now we have not contributed to public discussion of the central challenge to each of our three countries — pernicious inflation. Its causes are complex, and its effects are all-pervading. Inflation has become all the more baffling and distressing because it now co-exists with low rates of growth and relatively high unemployment.

Carl E. Beigie, president of the C. D. Howe Research Institute in Montreal and a member of the BNAC, agreed to take a fresh look at this subject for the Committee. This publication is Mr. Beigie's inquiry. We concur with the view he expresses: that control over inflation is a prerequisite to sustained progress in resolving most other economic problems. His argument — as the title implies — is that inflation does not arise only from incorrect economic diagnosis and therefore inappropriate policies, but springs rather from underlying socio-political realities and social expectations. Thus Mr. Beigie concludes that productive approaches to solutions must seek causes and remedies within the lifestyle of modern Western society itself through the gradual achievement of greater discipline within it.

His analysis points to the need for better understanding by the general public of the real choices available for dealing with inflation. The Committee is pleased to publish this report and to commend it for careful study.

Members of the Committee Signing the Statement

Chairmen
*SIR RICHARD DOBSON
President, B.A.T. Industries Limited

IAN MacGREGOR
General Partner, Lazard Frères & Co.,
Honorary Chairman, AMAX Inc.

Vice Chairman
SIR ALASTAIR DOWN
Chairman, Burmah Oil Company

Chairman, Executive Committee
WILLIAM I. M. TURNER, JR.
President and Chief Executive Officer,
Consolidated-Bathurst Inc.

Members
WILLIAM S. ANDERSON
Chairman of the Board, NCR Corporation

J. A. ARMSTRONG
Chairman and Chief Executive Officer,
Imperial Oil Limited

A. E. BALLOCH
Executive Vice President,
Bowater Incorporated

ROBERT A. BANDEEN
President and Chief Executive Officer,
Canadian National

SIR DONALD BARRON
Group Chairman, Rowntree Mackintosh
Limited

ROBERT BELGRAVE
Policy Adviser, British Petroleum Ltd.

I. H. STUART BLACK
Chairman, General Accident Fire and
Life Assurance Corporation Ltd.

JOHN F. BOOKOUT
President and Chief Executive Officer,
Shell Oil Company

JOHN F. BURLINGAME
Vice President and Group Executive,
International and Canadian Group,
General Electric Company

SIR CHARLES CARTER
Chairman of Research and Management
Committee, Policy Studies Institute

J. EDWIN CARTER
Chairman and Chief Executive Officer,
INCO Limited

SILAS S. CATHCART
Chairman & Chief Executive Officer,
Illinois Tool Works, Inc.

JAN COLLINS
Chairman, William Collins & Sons

KIT COPE
Overseas Director, Confederation of
British Industry

DONALD M. COX
Director and Senior Vice President,
Exxon Corporation

RALPH J. CRAWFORD, JR.
Vice Chairman of the Board, Wells Fargo
Bank

FRANK J. CUMMISKEY
IBM Vice President and President,
General Business Group/International,
IBM Corporation

DIRK DE BRUYNE
Managing Director, Royal Dutch/Shell
Group of Companies

JOHN DU CANE
Chairman and Managing Director,
Selection Trust Ltd.

GERRY EASTWOOD
General Secretary, Association of
Patternmakers and Allied Craftsmen

HARRY E. EKBLOM
Chairman and Chief Executive Officer,
European American Bancorp

J. K. FINLAYSON
Vice Chairman, The Royal Bank of
Canada

---

*See footnotes to the statement, p. 73.

Committee Signers

ROBERT M. FOWLER
Chairman, Executive Committee,
C. D. Howe Research Institute

MALCOLM GLENN
Executive Vice President, Reed Holdings
Inc., Reed International, Ltd.

HON. HENRY HANKEY
Director, Lloyds Bank International Ltd.

G. R. HEFFERNAN
President, Co-Steel International Ltd.

ROBERT HENDERSON
Chairman, Kleinwort Benson Ltd.

ROBERT P. HENDERSON
President and Chief Executive Officer,
Itek Corporation

JACK HENDLEY
General Manager (International),
Midland Bank Ltd.

HENDRIK S. HOUTHAKKER
Professor of Economics, Harvard
University

DEAN DONALD P. JACOBS
Graduate School of Management,
Northwestern University

JOHN V. JAMES
Chairman of the Board, President, and
Chief Executive Officer, Dresser
Industries, Inc.

GEORGE S. JOHNSTON
President, Scudder, Stevens & Clark

JOSEPH D. KEENAN
President, Union Label and Service
Trades Department, AFL-CIO

TOM KILLEFER
President, United States Trust Company
of New York

CURTIS M. KLAERNER
Executive Vice President and Director,
Mobil Oil Corporation

H. U. A. LAMBERT
Chairman,
Barclays Bank International Limited

HERBERT H. LANK
Hon. Director, Du Pont of Canada Ltd.

WILLIAM A. LIFFERS
Vice Chairman, American Cyanamid
Company

CARGILL MacMILLAN, JR.
Senior Vice President, Cargill Inc.

J. P. MANN
Deputy Chairman, United Biscuits
Holdings Ltd.

A. B. MARSHALL
Managing Director, P & O Steam
Navigation Company

WILLIAM J. McDONOUGH
Executive Vice President, International
Banking Department, The First National
Bank of Chicago

DONALD E. MEADS
Chairman and President,
Carver Associates

PATRICK MEANEY
Group Managing Director,
Thomas Tilling Limited

C. J. MEDBERRY, III
Chairman of the Board, BankAmerica
Corporation & Bank of America NT & SA

SIR PETER MENZIES
Welwyn, Herts

JOHN MILLER
President, National Planning Association

DEREK F. MITCHELL
Chairman & Chief Executive Officer,
BP Canada Limited

MALCOLM MOOS
Hackensack, Minnesota

KENNETH D. NADEN
President, National Council of Farm
Cooperatives

WILLIAM L. NAUMANN
Former Chairman of the Board,
Caterpillar Tractor Company

WILLIAM S. OGDEN
Executive Vice President,
The Chase Manhattan Bank, N.A.

BROUGHTON PIPKIN
Chairman, BICC Limited

*SIR RICHARD POWELL
Director, Hill Samuel Group Ltd.

J. G. PRENTICE
Chairman of the Board,
Canadian Forest Products, Ltd.

LOUIS PUTZE
Director and Consultant,
Rockwell International

BEN ROBERTS
Professor of Industrial Relations,
London School of Economics

HAROLD B. ROSE
Group Economic Adviser,
Barclays Bank Limited

DAVID SAINSBURY
Director of Finance, J. Sainsbury Ltd.

WILLIAM SALOMON
Managing Partner, Salomon Brothers

A. C. I. SAMUEL
Director General, International Group of
the National Association of Pesticide
Manufacturers

NATHANIEL SAMUELS
Vice Chairman, Kuhn Loeb Lehman
Brothers International, Chairman,
Louis Dreyfus Holding Company, Inc.

SIR FRANCIS SANDILANDS
Chairman, Commercial Union Assurance
Company, Limited

PETER F. SCOTT
Chairman, Provincial Insurance
Company Ltd.

ROBERT C. SEAMANS, JR.
Massachusetts Institute of Technology

LORD SEEBOHM
Chairman, Finance for Industry

THE EARL OF SELKIRK
President, Royal Central Asian Society

*JACOB SHEINKMAN
General Secretary-Treasurer,
Amalgamated Clothing and Textile
Workers' Union

LORD SHERFIELD
Chairman, Raytheon Europe
International Company

R. MICHAEL SHIELDS
Managing Director, Associated
Newspapers Group Ltd.

WILLIAM E. SIMON
New York, New York

E. NORMAN STAUB
Chairman and Chief Executive Officer,
The Northern Trust Company

RALPH I. STRAUS
New York, New York

JAMES A. SUMMER
Excelsior, Minnesota

HAROLD SWEATT
Honorary Chairman of the Board,
Honeywell, Inc.

SIR ROBERT TAYLOR
Deputy Chairman, Standard Chartered
Bank Ltd.

A. A. THORNBROUGH
Deputy Chairman and Chief Executive
Officer, Massey-Ferguson Limited

SIR MARK TURNER
Chairman, Rio Tinto-Zinc
Corporation Ltd.

JOHN W. TUTHILL
President, The Salzburg Seminar

W. O. TWAITS
Toronto, Ontario

MARTHA R. WALLACE
Executive Director and Director,
The Henry Luce Foundation, Inc.

RICHARD C. WARREN
Consultant, IBM Corporation

W. L. WEARLY
Chairman, Ingersoll-Rand Company

VISCOUNT WEIR
Chairman and Chief Executive,
The Weir Group Limited

SIR ERNEST WOODROOFE
Former Chairman, Unilever Ltd.

---

*See footnotes to the statement, p. 73.

Acknowledgments

The ideas presented in this monograph were developed and refined in the unusually stimulating environment provided by my colleagues at the C. D. Howe Research Institute. I thank all of them, and especially Judith Maxwell and Gennifer Sussman, who made valuable comments on drafts. I am also grateful to the many members of the British-North American Committee who shared with me their ideas about the issues discussed in this monograph and to the Committee's research directors, Sperry Lea and Simon Webley, who pointed out numerous weaknesses in the initial presentation. As is the case with all publications of the C. D. Howe Research Institute, Connie Parsons has applied her skills and patience in editing the manuscript. Despite all this assistance, weaknesses undoubtedly remain, for which I am entirely responsible.

I. The Search for Discipline

Over the past several years governments in most industrialized nations have been beset by high inflation, high unemployment, balance of payments difficulties, and large budgetary deficits. Some nations have been fortunate in avoiding one or two of these problems and a very few (West Germany and Switzerland would fit into this category) have fared much better than the average in all four areas. Aside from these exceptions, however, national economic performances around the world have generally been lackluster at best and highly distressing at worst. Moreover, while policies have been devised to generate improvement in one or two of the four problem areas, this improvement seems always to be at the cost of a further deterioration, at least temporarily, in the others.

In their search for a way out of their economic plights, governments in the industrial nations have followed broadly similar courses in domestic policies. During the late 1960s and early 1970s, these policies were generally erratic and reactive, reflecting a strategy that has come to be known as "fine tuning." Policy-makers had been led to believe they could keep an economy on a reasonably smooth course by frequent but moderate changes in policies in response to danger signals. But they learned that danger signals are difficult to see and interpret, economic forecasting being a very inexact science; that corrective measures are not easy to devise and implement; and that, once such measures are put in place, their impact is often unpredictable in magnitude and/or timing. On numerous occasions, fine-tuning measures have ended up aggravating the problems to which they were addressed.

For reasons described in Chapter II, there was a serious and rapid deterioration in economic performances by late 1973 and early 1974. Faced with a set of problems clearly different in magnitude from anything experienced in the post-Korean War period, policy-makers began to seek alternatives to fine tuning. This search has led to policy statements and governmental actions that emphasize a return to fundamentals in economic affairs, steadiness in the application of policy measures, and moderation in individual and collective expectations. But while the words of political leaders and economics officials in the various industrialized nations reflect similar views about the nature of current problems and solutions to them, the determination with which these solutions are pursued varies widely among countries. Meanwhile, unemployment and inflation remain high and, in a number of countries, are rising or threatening to rise further. As a result, pessimism abounds as people sense that their leaders have lost control over economic events and do not understand how to regain it.

This monograph focuses more on a diagnosis of why the industrialized nations have arrived at their current collective economic predicament than on how that predicament is to be resolved, although a general framework for pragmatic policy responses is provided in Chapter VI. The diagnosis rests on two major hypotheses: that inflation is the dominant weakness in current economic performances, and a cure for inflation is a precondition for the effective resolution of other economic problems plaguing the world scene; and that while economists can contribute to an understanding of the causes and the effects of inflation, the tenacity of the inflation problem reflects the socio-political environment that has gradually emerged in most industrialized nations over the past two decades or so.[1] These hypotheses explain the choice of the title of this monograph: *Inflation Is a Social Malady*.

Reference will be made so frequently in this monograph to the current approach to economic policy among industrialized nations, and to challenges to the success of that approach, that it is useful to describe briefly its essential characteristics at the outset.

Characteristics of Contemporary Economic Policy

Two words — discipline and gradualism — are central to a description of the strategy governments claim they are employing to address current economic problems.

Discipline is reflected in the targets against which most governments now acknowledge their monetary and fiscal policies should be evaluated. Policy-makers have become increasingly "monetarist" in their orientation over the past few years. The basic monetarist tenet is that inflation is a monetary phenomenon, so that strict regulation of the rate of growth in the money supply is a necessary condition for bringing inflation under control and keeping it there. During the era of fine tuning, many governments placed primary emphasis upon the level of domestic interest rates rather than upon money-supply growth rates. Upward pressures on interest rates were resisted because of their high visibility and political sensitivity, given their impact upon the cost of home ownership and purchases of consumer durables on credit, and because of their depressing effect on business investment.

In order to hold interest rates down during periods of excessive demand, central banks were forced to allow money-supply growth to accelerate. According to monetarists, such a policy is a sure prescription for higher inflation in the future, which will lead in turn to interest rate levels being higher than if greater discipline over money-supply growth had been maintained. The contemporary policy approach reflects the view that short-term fluctuations in interest rates, even if

---

[1] Economics has traditionally been defined as the study of how scarce resources are allocated among unlimited wants. The maintenance of expectations within realistic boundaries, which is the meaning of "discipline" as used in this monograph, is the fundamental test of a society's continued viability.

to uncomfortably high levels, must be tolerated as the cost of achieving moderation in money-supply growth and in inflation.

In the area of fiscal policy, acknowledgment of the need for greater discipline can be found in government statements of commitment to reduced budgetary deficits. Deficit financing by governments, it is argued, means that funds that would otherwise be available to finance private, output-expanding investment are "crowded out." The resulting competition for these funds tends to push up interest rates and to add to pressures on monetary authorities to allow the money supply to expand excessively.

The contemporary approach to fiscal policy, however, encompasses more than just an advocacy of reduced budgetary deficits. It is argued that, even if budgets were to be brought closer to balance, the level and the rate of growth of expenditures by government are important factors in the inflation process.

In contrast to the short-term focus of fine-tuning strategies, attention is now being paid to the need to finance long-term growth in government spending with equivalent increases in government revenues. The more rapid the growth in spending, the heavier the tax burden on income earners. Unless taxpayers perceive higher direct benefits from government-supplied services and therefore accept voluntarily a heavier tax load, they are likely to resist that burden by trying to pass it along to someone else (for example, their employers or their customers). The process thereby set in motion has become known as "tax-push" inflation.

Discipline in the form of greater restraint in government spending, with a specific minimum target of keeping the ratio of government expenditures (including redistributive transfers of income) to total output (GNP) from rising further over time, has become widely accepted as a prerequisite for the restoration of non-inflationary conditions.

Gradualism has tempered the pace at which discipline has been incorporated into monetary- and fiscal-policy actions. The consequences have been what appears to be a half-hearted approach to longer-term economic targets, policy measures that run the risk of being too little and too late, and a proclivity for adopting a new variant of fine tuning as the time period over which gradualism is supposed to achieve its promised results has been varied to serve political expediencies.

For example, whereas the long-term appropriateness of the "monetary rule" — that the money supply should grow at approximately the same rate at which an economy's output of goods and services can expand over time — has been widely proclaimed, implementation of that rule has so far generally been approached gingerly. With few exceptions, central banks have brought about only gradual reductions in the range within which money-supply growth rates are permitted to fluctuate in the short run (which has been the case in Canada), and commitment even to that course has been less than determined (as experience in Britain and the United States has demonstrated).

Similarly, the target of reduced budgetary deficits has been relaxed, at least implicitly, by evaluating budgets in terms of what expenditures and revenues would be at "reasonably full employment" in an economy. Large deficits are tolerated as long as recorded unemployment rates remain above what is regarded as a "reasonable" — meaning politically acceptable — longer-term level.

The one area where discipline was applied fairly quickly when a new strategy was adopted in the mid-1970s was in expenditure policy. Experience varies widely among the industrialized countries; but, in general, government-spending growth has been restrained in comparison with that which occurred during the second half of the 1960s and the early 1970s. Unfortunately, the private sector has been slow to take up the slack in demand caused by this restraint, and the results have been a very hesitant recovery in total demand and rising unemployment in the developed countries as a group. Given the current situation in the world economy, the fine-tuning approach would be to cut taxes as a stimulus to growth. Governments have cut taxes, but they have done so only moderately because of concern over the implications for near-term budgetary deficits and a fear that a too rapid stimulus would rekindle inflationary pressures.

An Uneasy Compromise

The combination of a stated commitment to greater discipline and a gradualistic approach to this discipline raises obvious questions about how determined governments really are to improve their economic performances. The cost of gradualism has been significant. Slow growth in output, continued inflation, and reported unemployment rates that remain high by postwar standards have persisted for nearly five years. All that governments seem able to do now is to hope that gradualism will produce enough progress in at least some key economic performance indicators that they will not be forced to change course prematurely because of slow improvement, and possibly even deterioration, in other indicators.[2]

---

[2] In this environment the terms "optimism" and "pessimism" have taken on unusual meanings. An optimist is one who believes the inflation rate will fall more rapidly than the unemployment rate will rise; a pessimist believes the rise in unemployment will outpace the improvement in the rate of inflation.

Why has this course been adopted? Some would argue that, faced with conflicting pressures and advice, governments found that gradualism provided a convenient framework within which they could continue to accommodate, essentially on an *ad hoc* basis, a fairly wide variety of demands from various interest groups. If governments were really serious about discipline, this line of reasoning goes, they would cut back the absolute level of expenditure rather than take the easier course of only paring down growth rates.

While there is probably some validity to this viewpoint, it is excessively harsh. The basic alternative to gradualism would have been an immediate shift in policy to arrive at ultimate monetary- and fiscal-policy targets very quickly. Given the circumstances existing in the mid-1970s, it is understandable that such a course was rejected. A dramatic shift in policy of this sort would have been perceived as carrying high risks of an even more serious economic downturn than was being experienced, with higher unemployment, at least temporarily. In that event, public reaction would probably have been intense (or so political leaders thought); and the predictable response would have been a backing down by government, the most likely result of which would have been a perpetuation of the "stop-go" policy cycle characteristic of the fine-tuning period, with unemployment and inflation alternating as the main policy concerns of the moment, and with both problems growing worse over time.

Therefore, gradualism in pursuit of discipline constituted a compromise. In order to bring unemployment and inflation down on a permanent basis, uncomfortable levels of both would have to be tolerated for several years.

Initially this compromise had fairly widespread public support. Those chiefly concerned about the necessity for a return to discipline were willing to tolerate gradualism because of a sensitivity to the risks of moving so rapidly to desirable long-term targets that the harsh short-term consequences might force governments to abandon discipline altogether. Those whose main concern was that governments should act to sustain full employment at all times were prepared to tolerate some temporary unemployment as a necessary concession to basic economic realities. Moreover, this compromise reflected a growing awareness that the fundamental trade-off facing society over time is not between a little less unemployment and a little more inflation, but between a lack of economic discipline and increasingly authoritarian measures to control the economy that would seriously jeopardize individual freedoms.

The problem now facing the industrialized world is that this compromise does not seem to be working, or at least not working fast enough to be sustainable. This observation provides the focal point for this monograph.

Summary of Contents

The reader will find that this monograph focuses on the industrialized nations as a group rather than on detailed case studies of the experience of individual countries. This decision was reached on the basis of two main considerations.

First, the economic problems facing the industrialized world are perceived by the author to reflect a common malady. While some countries have been more successful in attacking this malady than others, no country has been able to escape the consequence of a deteriorating economic situation in a world that has grown increasingly interdependent.

Second, there is a serious risk of losing sight of the fundamental causes of the common malady by concentrating on detailed symptoms in individual nations. At any point in time a nation may be doing better or worse in relation to particular performance indicators as policies are addressed to the politically most sensitive problems of the moment. But the issue examined here is why the steady deterioration in overall performance in most industrialized countries has been so exceedingly difficult to reverse. Those who are knowledgeable about the economies of specific countries should find that the following discussion deals with familiar territory.

The monograph proceeds through the following outline. The next chapter provides a brief overview of the global economic condition, with a technical appendix containing a fairly simple graphic representation of why there appears to have developed a threat of permanently higher inflation *and* unemployment than nations can possibly regard as acceptable over a protracted period of time. Chapter III contains an evaluation of "gradualism" and alternative "big-lever" policy prescriptions for dealing with this threat. The main danger points identified there concern difficulties arising in the transition during which these prescriptions are administered to economies in serious disequilibrium. The purpose of Chapter IV is to ask whether these prescriptions reflect a satisfactory diagnosis of what ails modern industrial economies. This discussion, focusing on structural problems and their impact on the distribution of incomes, leads to the conclusion that additional correctives are probably essential if a satisfactory overall economic performance is to be achieved. Various strands of earlier commentary concerning government intervention and its disincentive effects are pulled together in Chapter V. The concluding chapter is devoted to a review of some possible responses to the danger points identified in the preceding chapters.

While the approach employed is based upon a reasonably traditional economic foundation, it attempts to incorporate some — admittedly rudimentary — sensitivity to political and sociological considerations judged relevant to economic-policy analysis, since these considerations are regarded as essential to an understanding of the inflation malady. Therefore, commentary on institutional and behavioral factors is interspersed throughout the presentation. Moreover, whereas economic analysis tends to focus upon "comparative statics" — a methodology that examines two or more alternative situations without paying very much attention to adjustment processes — this monograph attempts to bring in some of the dynamic aspects involved in policy matters. This emphasis upon dynamics reflects a perception that problems encountered during a transition period usually provoke additional, and often unanticipated, policy reactions. As a result, the ultimate outcome of a particular policy initiative often turns out to be quite different from what was originally expected.

II. An Overview of the Global Economic Condition

High Expectations, Disappointing Performance

The global economic condition in the 1970s has been, and to a large extent remains, distressing. Inflation accelerated sharply in 1974 and 1975 and then subsided somewhat, but to levels well above those experienced in the 1960s and early 1970s. Progress in reducing inflation further has been grudging and erratic, and by mid-1978 a renewed acceleration came to be widely regarded as a near-term prospect. Moreover, the limited progress that has been made toward greater price stability has come at the cost of a serious recession, followed by persistent slow growth, with a significant rise in unemployment and in unused production capacity. Major imbalances also emerged in international economic transactions, contributing to growing protectionist attitudes and actions.

If comparisons are made with some earlier periods in economic history (the 1930s being an obvious example), performance in the 1970s might not be judged too harshly. But current performance is being evaluated not against the distant past, but against expectations generated in the 1960s. Those expectations were based both on the optimism of economists that business cycles could be kept within narrow boundaries by the application of "Keynesian" approaches to demand management and on the actual performance record during most of the 1960s, when solid growth was combined with declining rates of unemployment and reasonably stable prices. That record has not been sustained, and the world is groping for new approaches to extricate itself from its current economic plight.

Expectations, and the bases upon which a government's economic performance tends to be judged, are reflected in policy targets. Because targets are referred to throughout this monograph, it is appropriate to set out briefly here the dominant idealized performance targets, or "benchmarks," against which economic conditions have come to be evaluated.

Basic Economic Performance Targets

Most countries would subscribe to variants of four, or possibly five, basic economic performance targets, and some nations have embodied such targets in domestic legislation. These targets, and a brief comment on their conventional operational equivalent, are as follows:

Strong economic growth. In practice, this target, to be achieved through technological advance and rising productivity, used to be regarded as having been met if full employment and price stability were accomplished. The analytical tool for evaluating growth has now become "potential GNP." This is computed by, first, adding together the expected rate of growth in the labor force and a productivity growth factor (defined in terms of output per unit of labor input) calculated in relation to historical experience. This figure is then applied to output at a recent period of "full employment," to arrive at an estimate of potential GNP in a particular year. Actual GNP, adjusted for price changes, is then compared with potential GNP. The larger the gap between the two, the less satisfactory performance is judged to be.

Full employment. This target has been defined in terms of the rate of unemployment. No one regards a zero rate of unemployment as feasible or desirable, one reason being that unemployment, as it is measured, includes people who are between jobs and taking time to find the jobs they want. In North America, unemployment at about 4 percent of the labor force or less was regarded as a satisfactory performance in the 1960s, but in Western Europe and Japan that target figure was much lower.[1]

Reasonable price stability. The consumer (or retail) price index, which has come to be equated in the public's mind with the "cost of living," is the common benchmark here. The term "reasonable" translates into different rates of price advance in different countries. In North America, increases of 2 percent per annum used to be regarded as reflecting stability — because, it could be argued, the methods for measuring price changes produced recorded inflation where none in fact existed (for example, because of incomplete accounting for quality improvements). Other countries, however, would have regarded a 4-5 percent rate of price advance as reflecting "reasonable" stability, since the anticipated costs of trying to lower that rate significantly would have been too socially disruptive.

A viable balance of international transactions. One benchmark that has commonly been applied here is a stable external value for the national currency. Two problems have arisen with respect to this target, however, and they will be expanded upon later. One problem is that nations performing better than is necessary to sustain a stable currency are expected to experience a relative rise in the external value of their currencies. But such strong-currency nations usually resist such a rise because of internal pressures from exporters and from import-competing industries whose prospects are less favorable with an appreciating currency. The other problem is the tendency to expand the targets on external transactions to include specific objectives with

---

[1] There are many reasons for variations in target unemployment rates among various countries, including differences in industrial structure (for example, the importance of seasonal industries), in labor mobility, in societal preferences and institutions, and in the measurement of unemployment. The important point about these target rates is not that they differ among countries but that there be stability in the underlying labor-market conditions within a country over time.

respect to individual components of the overall balance of payments (for example, the trade account, the manufactured-products account, or, at an even narrower level, the technology-intensive-products account).

A more "equitable" distribution of income. While this target may not have the same degree of commitment in some countries as the four covered previously, governments everywhere are forced to pay attention to the impact of policy measures upon the distribution of income shares. However, it is extremely difficult to define a precise target in this area.[2] Total equality in incomes is not a practical goal, since it could be pursued only at the cost of very serious growth disincentives. Therefore, performance in this area tends to be judged in terms of the direction of change in the percentage of the population with incomes above some arbitrary, and constantly moving, "poverty line" or of the extent to which the dispersion of incomes narrows over time. Another type of problem arises when the income-distribution effects of policies are evaluated, as they often are, on the basis of which income groups provide tax revenue, without taking into full account the distribution of benefits from government spending programs.

Falling behind the Targets

During the first fifteen years of the postwar era, performance in relation to these targets was mixed. Severe, but temporary, bursts of inflation followed World War II and accompanied the Korean War. Business cycles continued to plague all nations, and balance of payments problems constrained flexibility in domestic policies. Growth accelerated as Western Europe and Japan recovered from wartime destruction and international linkages through trade and capital movements expanded. While simultaneous progress on all targets was rare, most governments could point to satisfactory performance with respect to at least one, and there was a sense that forward momentum would continue. (The 1950s were relatively lackluster years in North America, but they provided a period of calm in which the memories of the violent fluctuations of the pre-war years began to subside.)

The first half of the 1960s was a truly exceptional period in modern economic history for most industrialized countries. Output expanded rapidly, unemployment declined toward full-employment benchmark levels, and there was little serious deterioration on the inflation front. New social programs were launched that raised absolute incomes of the poor and other disadvantaged groups. The only early hint of a problem that might eventually mar this situation was the

---

[2] For a highly informative treatment of this topic, see Theodore Geiger, *Welfare and Efficiency: Their Interactions in Western Europe and Implications for International Economic Relations* (Washington, D.C.: National Planning Association, 1978).

emergence of persistent U.S. payments deficits, but it could be argued with reason that these deficits were appropriate in order to provide dollars to an international monetary system apparently short of reserves and that the strong international-net-worth position of the United States could easily support the mounting liquid short-term claims on that country.

During this brief period it appeared that the "new economics," based essentially on Keynesian prescriptions for demand management and on the concept of "fine tuning," had solved the problems of major business cycles and periodic bouts of high unemployment. The targets outlined above came to be regarded not as idealized goals that could never really be reached, but as firm performance standards that should be achieved.

Following the solid performance of the early 1960s, danger signals started flashing with increasing intensity during the second half of the decade. Even though output still grew rapidly, unemployment continued to decline, and social programs improved the well-being of more and more people, inflation started to rise and serious balance of payments difficulties became more frequent and widespread. Efforts to deal with these emerging problem areas made it more difficult to sustain performance with respect to other targets. It was at that point that a series of developments began that are still causing distress in the world economy.

Basic Causes of Economic Distress

Clearly, many factors are responsible for the current global economic condition. In an attempt to place these into some sort of systematic framework — and not incidentally to reinforce the credibility of orthodox policies — an elaborate interpretation has been articulated by traditionalist economists to try to explain why the world economy has reached its current state. Three dominant themes emerge from this interpretation: policy errors, exceptional shocks to the system, and inappropriate standards against which policy performance is assessed.[3]

A Brief Chronology of Postwar Economic Events

Certain developments prior to mid-1965 might be cited as factors contributing to emerging inflationary pressures in the second half of the 1960s, but the single most serious event was a decision by the United States to engage in a major expansion of its Vietnam War effort

---
[3] The most detailed elaboration of this interpretation is to be found in *Towards Full Employment and Price Stability* (Paris: Organisation for Economic Co-operation and Development, 1977). A summary and critique of this report, prepared by Gennifer Sussman, is included as an appendix to this monograph.

in 1965-66 without paying for the resulting increase in military expenditures by raising taxes or by cutting back other outlays, such as for an ambitious space program and major new social programs enacted under President Johnson.

The U.S. economy had gradually reached a delicate balance by the mid-1960s. Unemployment was down to below 4 percent, the consumer price index had been reasonably stable at about a 2 percent annual increase (with the wholesale price index having been essentially flat), and the balance of payments deficits were still widely regarded as manageable. But there was virtually no non-inflationary room left to meet the demands generated by a major new stimulus of the sort provided by Vietnam War expenditures. What followed was a classic case of "demand-pull" inflation.

Demand-pull inflation spills over into rising prices, higher interest rates, and increased imports and reduced exports. If the inflationary shock is large, and especially if it persists, the spillover is felt in labor markets. Large demand excesses create shortages everywhere. Selective wage rates are bid up as a reflection of shortages of workers, and this process spreads as traditional wage-rate relationships are restored. When institutional considerations such as long-term collective bargaining agreements that delay necessary adjustments are taken into account, the unwinding process from an initial inflationary shock can take several years to run its course.

There is a tendency to view this process as reflecting cost-push (usually read wage-push) inflation. This is an example of analysis based on symptoms rather than on root causes. Without the demand-pull inflation to start the cycle, the "catch-up" process need not have taken place. We will be returning to the catch-up issue later in this monograph.

It would have been easier to isolate the impact of excess demand in the United States if the world had been on a flexible-exchange-rate system at the time. The spillover of this excess demand into the trade sector would have been moderated by a depreciation in the relative value of the U.S. dollar. As a result of a fixed-exchange-rate system and of the fact that the U.S. dollar was the main source of international reserves, however, the spillover spread to other countries and added to the world's accumulation of liquid claims on the United States.[4] The rapid growth in these claims eventually led to a suspension of their

---

[4] The exchange-rate system at the time was based upon currencies pegged either to the U.S. dollar or to an ounce of gold. Although governments were required to maintain the value of their currencies within a narrow band around that peg, procedures existed whereby the peg could be increased or decreased. Instead of lifting the pegged value (revaluing) to head off the importing of U.S. excess demand pressures, most governments experiencing these pressures added to their holdings of U.S. dollars, thereby helping to finance the U.S. excesses.

convertibility into purchases of gold held by the United States and to the end of the fixed-exchange-rate system in 1973.

The inflationary surge would also have been better contained if money-supply growth rates had been more tightly controlled. But the short-term consequences of such an approach — higher interest rates and probably higher unemployment — were politically unpopular, so the U.S. war effort in Vietnam was, to a large extent, financed by the printing press.

As inflation rates began to rise in the late 1960s, governments responded with credit squeezes and tax increases, but their policy actions were delayed, half-hearted, and not sustained. There was too much concern about the unemployment consequences of anti-inflation measures to stick with them. Government expenditures continued to grow rapidly, fueling demand excesses, and the phenomenon of "stop-go" policies spread. Governments alternated frequently between anti-inflation ("stop") and anti-unemployment ("go") measures.

The situation came to a head in 1972-73. All major countries were simultaneously in a phase of expansion. The result was one of the most rapid increases in output — and more importantly, in demand — on a world basis in modern "peacetime" experience. (By then the Vietnam expenditures had essentially reached a plateau, from which they subsequently subsided.) Much attention was focused on supply shortages in this period, and there were bottlenecks and disruptions in selected commodity markets. However, generalized shortages were the natural consequences of widespread excess-demand inflation. When excess-demand problems subsequently subsided, so too did most of the concern about shortages.

Then came an approximately fourfold increase in the world price of oil in late 1973 and early 1974. This dramatic increase over such a short span of time had a significant impact on all general price indices, which were already rising rapidly. At the same time, higher oil prices had a deflationary impact on the world economy. Income taken away from consumers of oil was only partially reinjected into the spending stream by the oil exporters, at least in terms of direct expenditures. Thus OPEC nations experienced a massive increase in their combined current-account surpluses, and these surpluses had to be matched by equivalent deficits for the rest of the world. The OPEC surpluses were "recycled," but these funds (or petro-dollars) did little to expand the productive base of the world economy. Instead, the funds essentially went toward financing oil imports, the level of which was not very responsive to higher prices.

To recap briefly, the "oil shock" produced the following negative effects in terms of the policy targets described earlier:

- Inflation rates were given a further sharp boost.
- Balance of payments problems for certain oil-importing countries became severe.
- Growth rates in oil-importing nations were curtailed as purchasing power for non-energy items fell. (Some governments — for example, that of Japan — appear not to have been particularly disturbed to have excess-demand pressures thereby reduced.)
- Slower growth was reflected in rising rates of unemployment.
- Higher energy costs bore disproportionately on low-income groups, although policies were in many cases introduced to ease this burden.

The world economy went into a serious recession in 1974-75. Some domestic factors of production were unused as unemployment rates increased and capacity-utilization rates for plant and equipment fell. The conventional wisdom of the 1960s would have called for the infusion of stimulus through tax cuts and/or government spending increases to put these factors of production back to work. By 1974-75, however, most nations were so concerned about inflation, large budgetary deficits, and balance of payments problems that they found such a policy course impossible to justify.

The world economy gradually moved out of recession after 1975, but progress was slow and sporadic. By 1978, officials and some private forecasters claimed that a much better picture would begin to emerge in the near future. Other observers, and the majority of the general public, had a wait-and-see attitude. The remainder of this monograph suggests they may have a long wait.

Deviating from the "Proper Policy" Path

The preceding chronology makes clear that a major cause of the world's current economic distress is past policy errors resulting from either inadequate understanding of economic processes or political expediencies. Economists have identified a number of such errors, but three stand out.

First, *fiscal policies were too stimulative*. Government expenditures grew at an unsustainable pace, and policy-makers lacked the political will to finance these expenditures with higher taxes. Keynesian prescriptions were misused. Instead of employing fiscal policy to fill valleys and to shave peaks in private demand, new, long-term expenditure programs were introduced that filled valleys and added to peaks in an inflationary manner. Furthermore, even where revenues were increased to pay for these spending programs, inadequate attention was paid to the consequences in terms of "tax-push" (a variant of "cost-push") inflation.

Second, *monetary policies were allowed to become too expansionary.* When governments found that their spending was increasing too rapidly, it was easier to boost money-supply growth rates than to accept the political costs of making the difficult adjustments (tax increases and/or spending cuts) required. Thus monetary policy accommodated inflation, although in the majority of cases it probably was not the initial cause of inflation.

Third, *a fixed-exchange-rate regime was retained too long in the international monetary system.* Differential rates of inflation and productivity growth, together with structural variations in nations' trading patterns, made it impossible to defend rigidly fixed currency relationships. Some adjustments would have taken place if nations had varied their currencies within established IMF rules, but the pivotal role of the U.S. dollar created special problems when the United States allowed its external accounts to become seriously out of balance. The prescription that most other currencies should be revalued upward relative to the U.S. dollar was simply impractical in the environment that existed at the time. In an effort to resist such revaluations, many nations allowed their domestic money supplies to surge upward, thereby fueling the global inflationary process.

Exceptional Price Shocks

Policy errors have been of sufficient magnitude to create serious problems in and of themselves. In addition, however, a series of exceptional price shocks delivered a devasting body blow to the world economy. Three such shocks are singled out for attention here.

First, *when flexible exchange rates in the early 1970s were finally introduced, a major realignment resulted.* One outcome of this development was an additional new source of price increases in nations whose currencies declined in relative value. These price increases were of a "once-and-for-all" variety (whereas inflation is characterized by continuous price increases), but their total impact was magnified by their incorporation into domestic cost levels (for example, by cost-of-living adjustments to wages). A more subtle result arose because currency realignments of the sort that were experienced necessitated difficult domestic industrial adjustments. For example, in nations whose currencies appreciate in relative value, marginal export industries were no longer competitive, and resources had to be transferred to other sectors more oriented to supplying domestic customers. Such adjustments raise temporarily the rate of capital formation required to maintain full employment.

Second, *selected supply shortages developed,* the most serious of which took place in the food sector. The food story is a complicated one, involving adverse climate, output-restricting policies, and changing Soviet attitudes toward relying upon grain imports to meet demand when domestic production declines. The important point, though, is that supplies fell short of surging demand, inventories were depleted, and prices rose sharply. Subsequent events have again proven an old market dictum: short-term adjustments to supply problems take place first in prices; longer-term responses are focused on output. Even short-term supply problems, however, may have long-term price effects, and problems in the food sector may not be just temporary. Because cost-of-living adjustments have become so widespread and institutionalized in many countries, even temporary price increases tend to become embedded at least partially in long-term cost structures.

Third, and by far the most important, *energy cost increases have wrought havoc on the world economy.* OPEC's pricing policies clearly produced a shock, but recognition of the fact that this shock is by no means temporary has come slowly. OPEC's power ultimately resides in the fact that there are no inexpensive alternatives to the oil its members control. Oil-importing nations have made some adjustments in their energy-consumption habits, but progress in making the general public aware of the full consequences of higher energy costs in terms of living-standard expectations has been slow.

Inappropriate Policy Standards

Even in the absence of obvious policy errors and exceptional price shocks, it can be argued that the world economy would still be in a troubled condition today. The reasoning is that benchmarks set for policy targets on the basis of the experiences of the 1960s are inappropriate for the 1970s.

Consider, first, the target of *strong economic growth.* Referring back to the discussion of "potential GNP," two types of complications have arisen since the late 1960s. The productivity growth experienced in Western Europe and Japan during the previous decade, for example, was not a sound basis for trend extrapolation of potential in the 1970s. Exceptional productivity catch-up factors were included in that earlier period, and sooner or later an economy gets "caught up." On a broader scale, a number of structural considerations appear to have contributed to a slowing of productivity growth potential; these will be examined in Chapter IV.

The other complication was particularly significant in North America. Unusually rapid labor-force growth, which both Canada and the United States have been experiencing, lifts the potential rate of growth in an economy as it is conventionally calculated. This procedure assumes that labor-force growth and productivity growth (defined in terms of output per unit of labor input) are independent of each other. But that is not a very realistic assumption. Young workers and women entering the labor force for the first time, or after a lengthy period out of the labor force, cannot be expected to have the same productivity on the job initially as average workers with considerable seniority. Both these complications suggest that "potential GNP" is being overstated, and demand-management policies geared to such an overestimate of potential are inflationary.

The second target is *full employment*. Standards of performance appropriate for the 1960s have become inappropriate for the 1970s. Social programs have been introduced that were bound to raise the recorded rate of unemployment even if actual labor-market conditions did not change. For example, unemployment-benefit programs in some countries have encouraged people to spend a longer time searching for the "right" job, which raises the reported rate of unemployment. People who are undecided about labor-market participation have been provided with opportunities to enter the work force long enough to qualify for unemployment benefits.[5] The point is not that such social programs are undesirable, but that their impact should be taken into account in establishing full-employment-performance standards.

A related problem is that unemployment rates tell us nothing about employment growth. The more rapid the rate at which the labor force grows, the greater the need for increased capital formation to provide the plant and equipment required to employ workers efficiently. Therefore, full employment under these conditions cannot be assured by aggregate demand-management policies alone. Complementary developments — particularly adequate capital investment — must also take place.

Performance with respect to *price stability*, the third target, must be judged in relation to exceptional shocks. In the case of the sharp increase in oil prices, for example, inflation as measured by general price indices was almost certainly a necessary part of the adjustment process. The difficulty is that wages and other forms of income have become so tied to cost-of-living clauses, or at least to a "catch-up" mentality, that this form of adjustment has been blunted.

Stable exchange rates were never a particularly appropriate standard for the target of *balance of payments viability*; they have become less so. Exchange-rate flexibility is an essential market adjustment mechanism in a period of rapid and profound economic change. An alternative performance standard, balance on current-account transactions (trade in goods and services), is impossible to achieve for oil-importing nations as a group as long as OPEC surpluses persist.

---

[5] Michael Walker and Herbert Grubel, eds., *Unemployment Insurance: Global Evidence of Its Effects on Unemployment* (Vancouver: The Fraser Institute, 1978).

(These surpluses have now shrunk substantially.) No alternative standard has been agreed upon in this area, and this lack of agreement represents a serious threat to the international trading system.

Finally, any target relating to income distribution must be evaluated on the basis of standards that reflect the realities of slower growth during the 1970s in the amount of output that can be used to finance redistributive transfer payments. During the 1960s it was primarily growth in total output, rather than a significant redistribution of the shares of output, that increased the well-being of the poor and other disadvantaged groups.

A Framework for Policy Analysis

The preceding discussion has provided, in capsule form, a diagnosis of the major factors that have caused a deterioration in economic performance since the mid-1960s. There is little serious disagreement among a substantial majority of economists that each of the points raised is important, although any consensus on the relative ranking of them would be difficult to achieve. Furthermore, a number of other factors, such as the impact of government regulation, have been omitted; some of these will be taken up in later chapters.

Where economists disagree, or at least where the general public perceives sharp disagreement, is in the area of prescription rather than of diagnosis. Part of the disagreement lies in different analytical frameworks within which policy prescriptions are formulated. Therefore, it is appropriate to pause here to set forth the specific framework that underlies the analysis in the monograph.

The formal specification of this framework can be found in a technical note at the end of this chapter. It is an approach familiar to those acquainted with basic Keynesian methodology as taught in most introductory economics courses. The presentation is structured in such a way that inflationary forces are emphasized. By the introduction of some fairly reasonable assumptions and quite elementary dynamic considerations, however, a situation is generated in which both inflation *and* unemployment persist.

This framework is suggested because it takes into account the key problems characterizing contemporary economic systems. Specifically, it encompasses

- the inflationary consequences of a struggle for income shares
- constraints on the potential for supply expansion over time
- transfers of purchasing power from oil-importing to oil-exporting nations.

The role of money in this approach requires a brief comment. A key assumption is that excessive rates of growth in the money supply validate, but do not initiate, inflationary pressures. This is not an anti-monetarist approach and in no way implies a challenge to the policy prescription that moderation in money-supply growth is an essential precondition for a return to price stability. Rather, the assumption reflects a belief that monetary policy alone is unlikely to cure inflationary pressures originating in excessive income expectations and supply restraints. Furthermore, our perception is that, while monetary policy may influence expectations and supply factors, it takes a relatively long time to do so. As a result, there are serious questions about the political feasibility of government's maintaining the necessary degree of monetary restraint long enough to subdue inflation. Thus central bankers require the support of a wide-ranging policy attack on a variety of fronts if their task of keeping inflation under control is to be a manageable one.

Technical Note to Chapter II

Figure 1 is a variant of a tool familiar to any student who has taken a course in economics — the C + I + G diagram. The horizontal axis on this diagram records the real output of goods and services produced in an economy that is available for distribution to people and organizations residing within that economy. On the vertical axis are recorded the domestic uses to which that output is directed.

Let us assume that, at a particular point in time, there is a state of equilibrium in the economy in the following sense:

- All resources (labor and physical capital) are fully employed, so that actual output is equal to the economy's maximum sustainable potential.
- Output is fully distributed among consumption (C), government expenditure on goods and services (G), and investment (I), and users in all three categories are willing to accept as satisfactory their shares of domestic product.
- The economy is in a balanced position internationally, with imports equaling exports of goods and services.

This situation corresponds to point y_0^F in Figure 1 (with subscript 0 denoting a full-employment condition). Because this is an equilibrium situation, the money supply (which determines the absolute level of prices) is assumed not to be increasing at an inflationary rate.

The 45° line in Figure 1 corresponds to equilibrium between what an economy produces and what it spends. We are assuming that our hypothetical economy lies initially on that line. Let us now ask what problems might develop that would prevent this economy from remaining in equilibrium over some future time period, the end of which is designated by the subscript 1. If equilibrium could be sustained, we would find the economy, at the end of the time period, at point y_1^F on the horizontal axis in Figure 1. The distance between y_1^F and y_0^F is determined by the productivity with which net new entrants to the labor force are employed. (y_1^F divided by y_0^F defines both the actual and the potential growth rates of the economy for the period examined.)

We observe that the maintenance of constant shares of domestic output for consumption, of government spending on goods and services, and of investment *might* preserve a state of equilibrium. Constant shares are shown by extending the three sloped lines drawn from the origin. Consumption equal to $y_1^F A$, government spending equal to AB, and investment equal to BD (all measured by vertical distances) would mean the same distribution of output among domestic uses in period 1 as in period 0.

Suppose, however, that disequilibrating forces are set in motion that tend to alter these shares. As specific examples, suppose that:

FIGURE 1

A Model of the Inflation-Unemployment Process

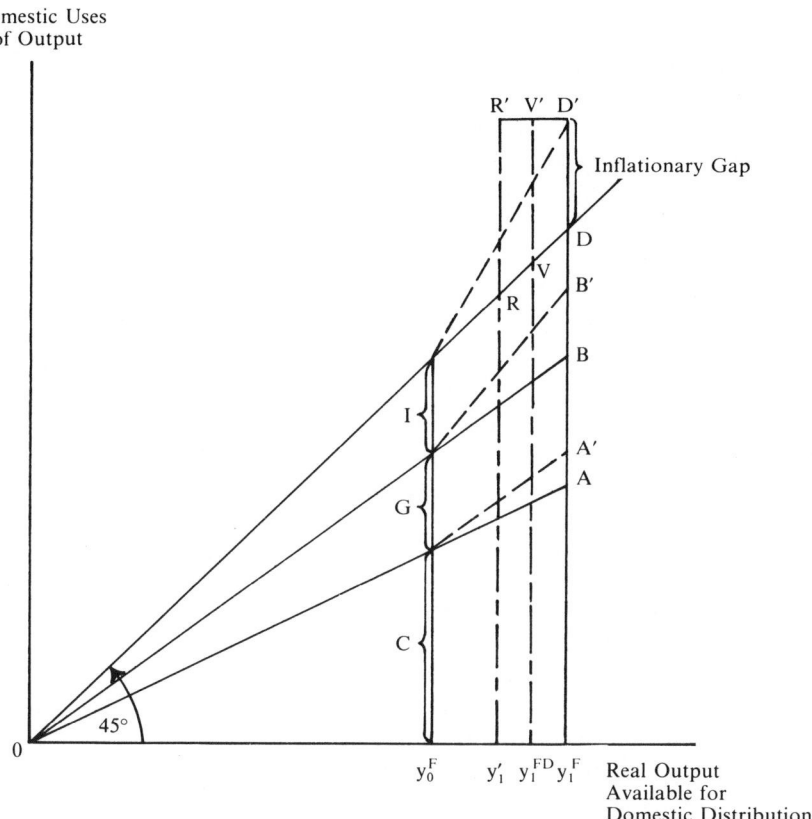

On the consumption side:

- The government transfers income to people who have a high propensity to spend, financing these transfers by taxes on those with a lower propensity to spend and/or by increased budgetary deficits (or reduced surpluses).
- Incomes, on average, increase at a rate in excess of productivity improvements.

On the government side:

- Expenditures under existing spending programs rise more rapidly than the rate of increase in domestic output.

- New spending programs are introduced that, in combination with existing programs, lead to total government spending's increasing faster than domestic output.

(We assume that any decline in consumption or investment brought about by higher taxes, by increased interest rates caused by deficit financing, or by a transfer of purchases from private to public sources of supply does not fully compensate for the increased government share of domestic output. Note that we are talking here of government expenditure on goods and services, exclusive of transfers. The impact of such transfers, in the framework employed here, is reflected in the private-consumption sector.)

On the investment side:

- There is a surge in the number of new entrants into the labor force, necessitating an increase in the share of output devoted to capital to maintain full employment at a constant capital/labor ratio. (This is known as "capital-widening" investment.)
- The amount of capital investment required to produce a unit of output rises, say because of the imposition of a stricter set of environmental standards.

Each of these factors tends to raise domestic demand on output available for distribution from domestic production. This tendency is reflected in the dashed lines in Figure 1, raising total demand at full employment in period 1 from D (an equilibrium level) to D' (a disequilibrium level). The distance between D' and D reflects an "inflationary gap." A sharp increase in the rate of growth of the money supply would be necessary to accommodate the inflationary process, but a restrictive monetary policy would not necessarily cure the root causes of this inflationary situation.

Two additional disequilibrating problem areas can be illustrated with this diagrammatic presentation.

First, suppose that the economy confronts a situation in which the cost of an essential import rises (the obvious example being oil) — that is, it takes more domestic output to obtain any particular volume of the imported product. If this increased import bill is to be offset by an increased volume of exports (the only alternatives are sales of the importing economy's assets or of claims on its future output), the real output available for *domestic* distribution in period 1 falls from y_1^F to y_1^{FD}. In the absence of a compensatory downward adjustment in the demands of domestic claimants on this output, the inflationary gap widens from DD' to VV'.

A change in the economy's external position — in technical terms, a deterioration in its terms of trade — has been posed this way

Technical Note to Chapter II

to demonstrate a critical point about the concept of "productivity" as it is normally perceived. In Figure 1, output between period 0 and period 1 has expanded from y_0^F to y_1^F. Dividing that increase by the labor force at the end of period 1 provides a commonly used measure of productivity gains. Part of that increased output, however, is not available for domestic distribution, since it must go to pay for higher-cost imports. The difficulty is that the "fairness" or "appropriateness" of claims for higher incomes is very often related to the measured "productivity" increase exclusive of the terms-of-trade-deterioration factor. If that is how income adjustments are actually made in practice, inflationary pressures are inevitable.

The second consideration arises from the fact that, while there may be an "inflationary gap," there is just so much output (possibly augmented in the short run by expanded net imports) available for domestic distribution. Suppose investment receives less than the necessary share of this output. Recall that the investment share has been defined in terms of the capital creation necessary to sustain conditions of full employment of the labor force. To the extent that other demands on output (consumption and government spending) "crowd out" this investment, actual output will fall below potential output. This is shown by a shift from y_1^{FD} to y_1'. This shift will translate into unemployment, and the inflationary gap will tend to rise further (to RR').

In conclusion, we have illustrated how an economy in equilibrium may move into a disequilibrium position characterized by higher inflation and higher unemployment. Depending upon the success of adjustment policies employed, this disequilibrium situation could persist for a considerable period of time.

III. Gradualism As a Policy for Restoring Equilibrium

The current commitment to greater discipline via the strategy of "gradualism," described in Chapter I, follows logically from the diagnosis that the global economic condition largely reflects past policy errors, as reviewed in Chapter II. Avoidance of obvious policy errors is an essential precondition for an improved economic performance around the world. At the same time, if the errors were serious and allowed to persist for some time, there are risks in trying to apply correctives too rapidly — hence the appeal of gradualism. But there are major questions surrounding the policy of gradualism, and the ultimate success of this strategy is by no means a certainty. Before turning to these questions, a brief commentary on the policy process will provide some necessary background.

Recognition of the Inevitable Comes Slowly

Inflation is the inevitable outcome of excessive rates of growth in the money supply. Expressed at this level of generality, that hypothesis would be accepted as valid by virtually the entire economics fraternity. The policy prescription that emerges from the hypothesis is clear: strict control over money-supply growth rates is essential to the maintenance of price stability in an economy. If we are to come to terms with inflation, we must seek to understand why most governments have failed to follow this prescription during recent long periods of monetary excesses.

One key to achieving this understanding lies in government's perception of what is necessary for its political survival. A conversion to "monetarism," where it has come about, has taken place only when politicians have sensed a threat to their tenure in power as a result of public reaction against the persistence of high rates of inflation. The political costs of a determined effort to restrain inflation are perceived as being high. It is far easier to respond affirmatively rather than negatively to pressures from various interest groups for spending programs that add to budgetary deficits. On the other hand, there are a variety of ways in which government can avoid having to resist these pressures, at least in the short run, thereby building up inflationary pressures that will break out later, possibly under a government formed by a different political party.

These apparently easy options include:
- Access to the printing press (through central-bank financing of budgetary deficits).
- Increased tax revenue, especially when income taxes are graduated and incomes are rising rapidly because of inflation. (This means a

tendency for tax revenue to rise as a percentage of real income, even with no changes in tax schedules.)
- Various types of spending programs to ease the impact of inflation on those especially hard hit and/or those mobilizing their demands for inflation protection most effectively.
- The ability to expand net imports and to finance them through loans from foreign lenders, government or private. In addition, with a flexible exchange rate a government can take advantage of the (temporarily) easy option of allowing a country's currency to fall on international money markets to prevent its external balance of payments position from deteriorating too badly or too rapidly.

In short, a government not wishing to make tough decisions was able, during the late 1960s and early 1970s, to find a range of routes for delaying the full consequences of being unable to meet overly optimistic public expectations or of a lack of discipline in its own actions. The danger exists that, for some governments, gradualism may represent another escape route for the short run.

Periodic exercises in monetary restraint occurred often in the late 1960s and early 1970s, but in each case it was not long before public concern about inflation shifted to concern about performance in relation to other economic-policy targets, particularly unemployment rates. Reactions by policy-makers to relatively rapid changes in public concerns produced stop-go economic policies.

Is the situation really any different today? If so, how long do policy-makers have before there is yet another change in public attitudes? In an economy where the vast majority of people in the labor force are employed — which is the case even when unemployment rates are relatively high — one would expect inflation always to be a concern. Unemployment, in contrast, generates general public unrest primarily when it is rising, irrespective of the level. With more workers' being laid off, the danger always exists that you are next. Over the past few years, unemployment has risen, and as a result concern has been aroused. Yet the level of general unrest appears surprisingly subdued in comparison with similar periods of unemployment in the postwar era. One reason for this difference appears to be that recent inflationary experience has been so unnerving that people are willing to tolerate unemployment (as long as it hits someone else) in order to bring inflation under control. There is also a spreading perception (or convenient rationalization) that unemployment today is less serious a hardship to the unemployed because of expanded social welfare programs.

Public patience is limited, however, and therein lies the most serious risk to gradualism. Unless steady progress in reducing inflation is readily apparent, politicians will be under increasing pressure to adopt some new strategy, and the alternatives that have been put forward — such as harsh controls to curb inflation and massive new government expenditures to stimulate growth and employment — are distinctly unattractive. That public patience is already wearing thin can be seen in the marked increase in pressures for, and concessions to, trade protectionism, a course reflecting efforts to push an economy's domestic problems onto its trading partners.

Government policy-makers appear to be handling a potentially explosive situation somewhat casually at the moment. Gradualism has the ring of an action program to it, but it could easily turn into a strategy for inaction on a number of fronts requiring immediate attention, some of which will be explored in Chapter IV. In the remainder of this chapter, the strategy of gradualism itself is assessed in terms of certain "danger points" in its application.

Gradualism versus "Fine Tuning"

To hurt an economist's feelings these days, accuse him or her of advocating policies of "fine tuning" the economy. Fine tuning is a synonym for activism by government in the form of intervening frequently to change the "big-lever" policies — monetary and fiscal policies — to offset cyclical and random disturbances to economic equilibrium.

Fine tuning has earned a bad reputation among many economic-policy commentators because:

- The impacts of policy changes occur with long and variable lags and often produce unpredictable side effects. For example, reductions in taxes may show up in higher saving rather than higher consumption in periods of economic slack and high inflation.
- Forecasting the need for policy action, either in direction or amount, has proven increasingly difficult.
- While countercyclical arguments can be advanced in support of increased government spending, such spending too often has had the effect of raising government's share of total output over the entire cycle.

For these and other reasons, there is a growing body of support for the view that fine tuning is more likely to cause a worse situation, and that cyclical and random disturbances should be allowed to work themselves out. Therefore, the policy advice goes, put the big policy levers at an appropriate setting and leave them alone. Such settings would include money supply's growing at about the rate of potential output in an economy and government expenditure's growing at roughly the same rate.

Gradualism reflects, in large measure, this notion of the importance of proper long-term "dial" positions. The problem, however, is that the advice concerning the money-supply dial is to ease it back gradually. The temptation to fiddle with this easing-back process may be overwhelming if policy-makers are unable fully to convince the public (or themselves) that it is not their responsibility always to be doing something when progress on performance indicators is judged unsatisfactory over a particular period of time. In that event, gradualism will simply produce a new variant of fine tuning.

Policy-makers, reflecting the publics they serve, are prone to fads. In some respects the current criticism of so-called Keynesian fine tuning is one such fad. A degree of flexibility and adaptability is essential to sound policy formation. But there are occasions, and we would argue that many industrialized countries are in the midst of one now, when economic performance deteriorates beyond the limits within which moderate amounts of tinkering can help. The difficulty is that gradualism, an approach with virtually no parallel in economic history, may be inadequate to bring economies back within those limits. We now turn to some of the reasons for skepticism.

Monetary-Policy Mechanics

The basic logic of a gradual, rather than an immediate, move to a long-term target range for money-supply growth is that it takes time to neutralize built-up inflationary pressures and expectations. If the time path taken to this target range is too gradual, more inflation is experienced than is necessary to keep unemployment within politically tolerable limits, and inflationary expectations may become more deeply entrenched. Too rapid a time path may not allow enough financial room in the near term for sufficient real growth to keep unemployment from rising excessively and will therefore increase the risks of a policy flip-flop in a dash to employment generation. Economists have yet to demonstrate a capacity to estimate the optimal time path with any precision.

Even if the correct time path could be specified, monetary analysts have difficulty answering with precision two questions: What constitutes money? Is the rate at which money changes hands (its velocity) stable, or at least predictable? Given existing knowledge, it would be advisable to allow monetary authorities some discretion in their application of the principle of gradual restraint, but the danger will always exist that discretion will result in additional policy errors. What seems clear is that, no matter how money is defined, unless the growth of the money supply is brought down steadily, inflation will not be reduced significantly from present levels.

Another problem with mechanics arises concerning an appropriate base level of inflation toward which to strive. A notion appears to be spreading among some economists and policy-makers, at least in North America, that something in the range of a 5-6 percent annual increase in the consumer (or retail) price index is the best that can be achieved over the medium-term future. Given that some prices (for example, for fuels) must rise and that other prices are difficult to reduce, there is some logic to this argument. Furthermore, if a lower target inflation rate were perceived to require an "unacceptably" high level of unemployment, a strong case could be made, in terms of real costs and benefits, for opting for moderate inflation and a better unemployment performance. But how can we assure that a strategy of living with moderate inflation will not translate effectively into a reality of having to accept progressively higher inflation? It is unlikely we can.

"Living with" a particular inflation rate, even if "only" 5 percent, encourages everyone to seek protection from that inflation in terms of the incomes they receive. This process is likely to establish 5 percent as the floor, rather than the ceiling, for future inflation. But that will not be the final outcome. Future price shocks will boost the inflation rate from the 5 percent floor and will generate pressures to "live with" an even higher floor. At a more fundamental level, long-term inflation results from an economy's inability to reconcile income demands with its production potential. Therefore, if the required degree of social discipline is absent, the notion that a moderately high rate of inflation can be a stable rate will be an illusion.

This discussion of monetary-policy matters has been carried far enough for our purposes. The conclusions that emerge generally support monetarist policy prescriptions:

• A return to reasonable price stability that will be sustained over time is impossible if money-supply growth rates continue to be anywhere near as excessive as those experienced in most domestic economies in recent years.

• While the determination of the precise money-supply growth rate compatible with reasonable price stability over time is a complex exercise, movement toward this rate should be at a pace that places real pressure on the current inflationary process, even at the risk of some further extension of the present period of slow economic growth. Otherwise, excessive money-supply growth rates are likely to perpetuate an environment in which disequilibrium pressures and policies are addressed at too leisurely a pace. In specific terms, this conclusion translates into a prescription that the money-supply growth rate, appropriately defined, should be reduced each year as long as infla-

tion rates persist above a "reasonable" level, barring some major new shock such as the OPEC price increases of 1973-74.
- In defining "reasonable" price stability, an inflation target should be set as low as possible. The notion that a significant increase in the "base rate" of inflation must now be tolerated should be rejected. There cannot be an effective compromise that will work over any lengthy time span. This rejection should be stated explicitly and clearly by national political leaders.

It is an easy task to make a set of recommendations of this sort. In the remainder of this chapter and in the next two chapters, the much harder task of coming up with policies in other areas that will give these recommendations a realistic prospect of being following is tackled.

Fiscal-Policy Uncertainties

As has already been noted at several points in this monograph, monetary restraint applied with moderation is the essence of gradualism. If monetary restraint is to be pursued successfully, however, it is imperative to apply fiscal policies that support this approach. Unfortunately, there are a number of uncertainties in determining the proper use of government taxation and expenditure policies to meet this objective. These uncertainties fall into two categories: those relating to an economy clearly in disequilibrium and those relating to maintaining an economy in a state of general equilibrium.

Policies for Restoring Equilibrium

In the technical note to Chapter II a disequilibrium situation is described as one exhibiting an inflationary gap in the sense of demand exceeding supply for a fully employed economy. As part of the strategy of gradualism, governments have committed themselves to restraining the rate of increase in their expenditures. To the extent they have honored this commitment, the inflationary gap has been relieved. At the same time, however, spending restraint has contributed to at least a temporary increase in unemployment. Private sector demand has been sluggish as well, and governments are under increasing pressures to boost their spending to close the current demand gap.

The problem is basically that we have no general theory of disequilibrium economics to provide clear guidelines for getting out of the current economic difficulties. What we do know, with some reasonable assurance, is the following:
- With idle capacity and sharply higher investment costs, firms are reluctant to build ahead of demand, especially where uncertainties

about future growth rates, inflation rates, government policies, and international competitiveness abound.
- Consumers appear to react to high and uncertain rates of inflation and to concerns about future prospects by increasing the rate at which they are saving out of disposable income.
- Slow growth and protectionist policies have restricted import expansion and blunted opportunities for export-led growth.

There is a presumption that, as gradualism begins to show success, these sources of slack demand will correct themselves. Savings rates will come down, leading to increased private consumption; investment in the private sector will pick up; and nations will be less constrained in their approaches to import growth. The major uncertainty, indeed the dilemma, facing policy-makers today is whether these trends will begin to develop soon enough so that further increases in unemployment rates can be avoided. If not, the whole strategy of gradualism will be in jeopardy.

Policies for Maintaining Equilibrium

It is a common perception that rapid growth in government expenditure has contributed significantly to the development of an inflationary gap over the late 1960s and early 1970s. If this is indeed the case, and the evidence is persuasive, the restoration and maintenance of equilibrium may require a decline in the share of domestic output currently accounted for by the government sector. Yet to date most governments have made commitments that will, at best, keep current shares relatively constant over time. These commitments, even if fulfilled, mean that private consumption and/or investment will receive a smaller share of output than was received prior to the rise in government's share.

Sound fiscal-policy formation requires a careful assessment of the different sources of growth in government expenditure, a topic explored further in Chapter V. The point taken up here relates to a major uncertainty about appropriate guidelines for fiscal policy.

A popular concept for assessing the impact of fiscal policy is the budgetary position that should accompany full employment. In calculating this position, government expenditures and revenues are estimated on the basis of what they would be if the economy were operating at full employment. It is assumed, for purposes of this calculation, that expenditure programs and tax rates are fixed. The difference between these hypothetical expenditures and revenues is then computed to determine the full-employment budgetary position. Changes in this position are used to evaluate whether government fiscal policies have become more or less stimulative over a period of time. Thus, if the actual budgetary position registers an increased deficit, as would occur if unemployment rises, this would not be regarded as reflecting more stimulative government policies *unless* there was also a larger deficit as recorded by the full-employment measure of the budgetary position.

This concept appears appealing, but its application involves a number of complications. Three of these complications are cited below:

- A reasonable definition of full employment is necessary. If 4 percent unemployment, say, is the benchmark used, whereas the more appropriate benchmark is, say, 6 percent, then a constant full-employment budgetary position would, in fact, be stimulative. This problem may characterize the current approach to fiscal policy in the United States.

- There is limited guidance for policy-makers as to what is the appropriate level for a full-employment budgetary position. Should it record a surplus, a deficit, or a balance between receipts and expenditures? Does it matter if there is, say, a balance at one level of expenditures versus another?

- Unless the prescription is that the full-employment budgetary position should always be in balance (the arguments for which rest on numerous simplifying assumptions), should the same guidelines be applied at all times? Suppose there is a long-term upward shift in personal-savings preferences (in which case governments may have to save less or run larger deficits to maintain full employment). Or suppose there is an upward shift in the amount of private investment necessary to sustain full-employment equilibrium (in which case governments may have to run surpluses or smaller deficits).

The main conclusion to be drawn from this brief discussion is that simple fiscal-policy "rules" should be treated with skepticism. Advice always to balance budgets, to balance full-employment budgets, or to balance budgets over an entire business cycle comes from analysts more familiar with diagrams and simplifying assumptions than with the task of keeping a complex economy moving along a path of equilibrium.

A Partial Policy Resolution

In the preceding section of this chapter three general monetary-policy guidelines were put forward for a period in which an attempt is being made to restore equilibrium conditions. Some similarly general guidelines for fiscal policy are now proposed:

- Little purpose is served by allowing further increases in unemployment rates in most countries (the situation in the United States as of late 1978 is somewhat unique) unless income gains become more inflationary over time. (As will be argued later, economic slack appears to be the only practical way of restraining inflationary income demands.) If credible forecasts suggest such a tendency for unemployment rates to rise, stimulus is appropriate to prevent that outcome. Stimulus over and above that required to prevent the unemployment rate from rising further should be approached cautiously and should be conditional upon clear evidence of a reduction in inflationary income claims. The most serious challenge to the restoration of economic discipline is that unemployment rates will reach levels where pressures on politicians to abandon discipline will prove overwhelming.

- Given the persistence of widespread inflationary pressures, any stimulus from fiscal policy should take the form of tax cuts rather than increases in government spending as a share of total output. Tax cuts will, however, increase budgetary deficits, at least in the short run. Therefore, tax cuts should be accompanied by a firm program for further near-term reductions in overall expenditure by government if aggravation of the inflationary gap is to be avoided.

- Tax cuts should be employed for strategic purposes as opposed to simply providing general stimulus. The appropriate strategic purposes will vary among countries according to the specific set of problems each faces. For example, they might be used to particularly good effect in countering inflationary pressures if a government could obtain assurances from labor leaders that increased effective purchasing power, resulting from reductions in income taxes, would be reflected in lower wage demands in future collective-bargaining negotiations, a technique used to some effect in 1977 in the United Kingdom.[1]

- Consistent with restraint in overall government spending, serious consideration must be given to changing the mix in spending to favor output-expanding infrastructure investment. This point is explored further in later chapters.

---

[1] A difficult question concerning fiscal-policy formation at present is the form tax cuts should take if the goal is to encourage restraint in inflationary income demands. Cuts in sales taxes would show up immediately in lower reported rates of inflation and might help reduce expectations of future inflation. But such tax cuts may give rise to claims that they are not being fully passed along in the prices consumers must pay and may not have as strong an impact on income demands as would a direct cut in income taxes. Another major question is whether tax cuts should be aimed first at encouraging consumption or investment. Increased investment incentives would eventually stimulate consumption, but supply would expand to meet this demand. If significant selective shortages exist, incentives to reduce these shortages would be an obvious fiscal-policy priority.

Conclusion

Gradualism as an approach to bringing about a return of economic discipline makes a great deal of sense and should be supported as a pragmatic response to current economic problems. Application of this approach, however, inevitably involves a substantial element of discretion in the development of appropriate monetary and fiscal policies. If this discretion is used unwisely, gradualism will have become just another catch phrase behind which policy errors persist. The purpose of this chapter has been to provide a somewhat more concrete set of guidelines against which the strategy of gradualism can be evaluated than those contained in highly general statements of policy by governments.

Gradualism in the use of big policy levers, however, is unlikely to cure all the disequilibrium symptoms of the current economic situation — or will cure them only over a very protracted period of time. Progress would be quicker, and prospects for eventual success greater, if a series of complementary, and highly specific, actions were also undertaken. Chapter IV addresses problems giving rise to the need for such actions.

IV. Structural Problems and Their Impacts

The term "structural" is applied to a wide variety of economic problems and policy issues that have become matters of interest and concern during the 1970s. In order to give the discussion of this subject a degree of organization, these problems and issues will be grouped under three headings: adjustment rigidities, investment constraints, and efficiency handicaps. There are a large number of factors that might be included under each of these headings; the approach here will be to select some of the most important for brief examination. The reader should bear in mind that the full consequences of each of the specific factors discussed spill over into other heading areas.

Adjustment Rigidities

Four apparently dissimilar developments in the 1960s and 1970s can be analyzed within the same basic theoretical framework, outlined in the technical note to Chapter II. They are:

The rise in energy prices and costs. Energy prices have risen much more rapidly than any general price index since late 1973, and there is little likelihood that the real price of energy will fall significantly in the future.[1] Therefore, energy consumers are going to be relatively poorer than they were prior to the price increase, to an extent determined by the amount of energy consumption that continues after adjustment of spending patterns. This does not necessarily mean that all energy producers will be richer. For some, unit costs may have risen as much as unit revenues, but this is really a different issue from the one being examined here.

The increased share of government spending as a percentage of total output. The rise in government spending relative to total output means that purchasing power has been transferred from private to public consumption. This shift need not mean that consumers, as a group, are any worse off than prior to the shift. They will be, however, if public provision of goods and services is less efficient than private provision or if public goods that individuals would not purchase voluntarily in free markets are supplied to them. Also, to the extent government spending programs involve income redistribution, some are gainers at others' expense.

Stricter environmental regulations. The pursuit of higher levels of environmental quality means costs as well as benefits for an economy. Cleaner air and water represent benefits; costs take the form of a reduction in the potential output of physical goods and services.

---

[1] The "real" cost of oil has fallen modestly over the past several years as the U.S.-dollar price quoted by OPEC has stabilized at the same time that general inflation has persisted. For countries with appreciating currencies, the real cost of oil imports has declined even further.

Reductions in effective hours of work. Increases in the number of holidays, sick leave, and so forth, have reduced the number of hours worked per year per employee. Early retirement reduces the number of hours worked during the course of an employee's active work life. These reductions cut back potential output, although not necessarily on an exactly proportionate basis. One more day off on holiday, for example, reduces the number of effective working hours a year by one-half of one percent. If an economy generates about 2 percent annual productivity improvement per worker over time, this reduction amounts to roughly one-quarter of that potential improvement for one year.[2]

What ties these developments together is that they all contribute to a reduction in domestic output available for distribution to the domestic private sector. This reduction is being strongly resisted by all income earners, with inflationary consequences. Unless this resistance is overcome, or output available to the private sector is expanded, gradualism is destined to produce disappointment, since it will not really restore discipline.

Traditional methods of adjusting to the types of developments outlined above are blunted by a number of institutional and behavioral factors, most significant of which is the increasingly widespread use of cost-of-living adjustments (COLAs).[3] If prices rise because of, say, higher energy costs and stricter environmental standards, COLAs protect incomes from bearing the full burden of these costs, and the costs are passed on in the form of higher prices. If tax increases are used to finance higher government spending and these taxes show up in the final prices of goods and services, COLAs also take this into account, with the same result. And if an economy's inflationary excesses result in a fall in the international value of that economy's currency, higher import prices will also figure in COLA compensation.

A second source of rigidity arises from the fact that many types of government expenditure are also "indexed" to the general rate of inflation, either *de jure* in legislation or *de facto* in actual budgetary practice. Therefore, inflation's impact on the government's share of total real spending has been limited.

The third, and final, source of rigidity to be taken into account here is more complex. If income earners base their demands on after-tax receipts and/or on expectations of real increases similar to those

---

[2] This discussion suggests one reason why "potential" output is such a slippery concept. In calculating potential, some assumptions are essential regarding the continuation of existing institutional factors, such as the average work week.
[3] The issue here is not simply the existence of formalized COLAs, many of which do not provide full protection against reported inflation, but also the spread of an inflation-adjusted mentality, whereby protection against inflation is viewed virtually as a right.

they have acquired in the past, adjustments to changes of the type listed above are further constrained.

The orthodox economist's response to this line of reasoning is that expectations and behavior will change if the economy is subjected to policies that produce significant slack in terms of potential output. In short, unemployment will solve the problems. This is, in fact, the unstated assumption behind the policy of gradualism. There are at least three major "danger points" in this response.

First, social programs to assist the unemployed have generally become more generous in the past decade or so. Unemployment still causes serious hardship for some, but increased benefits appear to blunt the restraint on income demands that might have been expected from a given level of unemployment in a period when benefits were not as great. Similarly, the increased incidence of families having more than one income earner, at least in North America, may also reduce the restraining impact of higher unemployment. As a result of these and other factors, the amount of unemployment and the resulting loss of output needed to make a major dent in adjustment rigidities may well be so great that no government could tolerate them and remain in office.

Second, even if the adjustment rigidities were loosened by the consequences of slack markets, there is no guarantee that expectations would not remain latent, to burst out in very large increases in income demands when the slack eased. The hope of gradualists appears to lie in dragging the slack out long enough so that, by the time it is over, original expectations are forgotten.

Third, the last defense rests with those absorbing income claims. Sooner or later, the argument goes, those paying excessive claims will realize that their future viability is at stake and will resist these claims vigorously. This is a credible argument, but only if there is a perception that government will not be there to "bail out" the situation with subsidies, protection, and so on. That perception has not been encouraged by many governments in recent years.

Investment Constraints

When the question is asked: Who pays for the necessary adjustments noted above?, one looks around for a sector of the economy that is not "indexed" to inflation. The most general answer is private capital. Capital formation is based on a crucial expectation — a sufficient after-tax rate of return to cover the costs of new investment. If that expectation is not fulfilled, new investment outlays cease. The result is slower rates of output growth, higher unemployment, and increased inflationary pressures. This line of argument, outlined in the discussion of the diagram in the technical note to Chapter II, is fairly convincing in relation to the current world economic scene.

This issue is, of course, the subject of very heated debate. The basic rebuttal to the investment-shortage argument takes two forms — empirical and theoretical.

The empirical case rests on several observations. It can be argued, for example, that savings rates have been relatively high in recent years. One could therefore attribute continuing slow growth to inadequate demand caused by investment's falling short of planned savings. Another observation is that capacity-utilization rates remain depressed, in which case investment demand would naturally be restrained. Finally, by focusing on reported rates of return on capital, one gets the impression they are high in relation to the past and should generate a favorable climate for future investment demand.

The problem with conclusions based on these observations is as follows: The excess of potential savings over actual investment, as well as the existence of unutilized production capacity, *describes* a slow-growth, underemployed economy — it does not *explain* the current situation. Also, rates of profitability that are often cited measure returns to capacity already in place, but they bear no relation to what will be required to augment (or replace) an economy's capital stock at today's much higher costs.

The theoretical case made against the notion of investment shortages is based on the assertion that, if capital formation turns out to be inadequate, the rate of return on investment will rise until a satisfactory amount of investment funding is achieved. Furthermore, it is argued that other factors of production (especially labor) can be substituted for capital, and will be if capital's relative cost rises.

While the theoretical case is valid, its applicability must be considered in relation to the following factors:

- In many applications, the technological possibilities for factor substitution (labor for capital, for example) are limited, especially when international competitive factors, such as much lower labor costs in newly industrializing countries, are taken into account.

- The capital required to meet new environmental standards and to convert from one type of energy consumption to another makes only a limited contribution, at best, to output potential. Yet investment of this sort increasingly must have first claim on a firm's capital budget. Such higher capital costs must also be reflected in prices charged; if they are not, it will be impossible to justify new investment projects.[4]

---
[4] Environmental protection costs will have to be reflected in higher prices or investment will stop. Energy conversion costs may end up simply as windfall losses for owners of existing capi-

- The threat of price or profit controls inhibits any necessary rise in the rate of return on capital from occurring. (In some countries, there is also the threat of nationalization, or at least of forced price reductions, if reported profits, including a major inflation component, are perceived as being "too high.")

Only the passage of time will prove conclusively the seriousness of the investment-shortage issue. But increased capital formation appears to be an important part of the solution to virtually every economic problem being discussed. If policy-makers guess wrong in their approach to the shortage issue, and assume it is not serious when in fact it is, there will be far-reaching consequences in terms of a nation's ability to achieve its basic economic and social goals.

This section concludes with a partial list of reasons why the share of current potential output going to capital expansion may have to rise significantly above past trend lines.

- The task of meeting the energy needs of the industrialized world will create massive demands on financial markets. Conservation in energy consumption is an essential component of any effective energy policy, but many forms of conservation are capital-intensive. As examples, consider the initial capital costs of improving home insulation or of providing more energy-efficient means of moving people to and from, and within, urban centers. Conservation alone, however, will not solve the energy problems facing the world economy. New production sources must be found and developed, and the capital requirements involved will be extraordinary. Consider one example that is by no means extreme: The capital costs of the Syncrude operation for extracting oil from the Alberta oil sands will exceed $2 billion. Output from the project will amount to 125,000 barrels a day. Thus it will cost more than $16,000 to install one barrel a day of new production capacity. Four barrels a day of capacity (excluding refining) requires about as much capital (more than $64,000) as a moderate-sized house in North America. Yet the average North American driver consumes roughly that much fuel (about 144 gallons) in three months. This energy is replacing depleting oil reserves in conventional fields that cost only a fraction as much capital to bring into production.
- A rise in labor-force growth rates requires a temporary increase in the rate of investment to sustain a steady capital/labor ratio.
- Marked changes in exchange-rate relationships among major currencies and in fuel costs may have accelerated the need to re-

---

tal without discouraging future investment prospects. In both cases, these costs reflect higher demand for capital.

place existing capital facilities that are no longer economic under these changed conditions.
- Clean air, clean water, safe working conditions, and so forth, are social goals that in many cases can be achieved only through increased capital investment.

Capital "shortages" always exist, in the sense that more investment can be placed at positive real rates of return than funds are available to finance. Therefore, some mechanism must exist to set priorities among competing uses. Market rates of interest provide one such mechanism, but inflation distorts the manner in which that mechanism operates. For example, inflation tends to channel funds toward traditional inflationary "hedges" (such as gold, land, and paintings) rather than toward capital formation that will expand a nation's output base.

Another problem area in contemporary capital markets arises from heavy borrowing by governments to meet budgetary deficits and from the granting by governments of various preferences in obtaining funds to different groups of borrowers, such as home-buyers. As a result of this government borrowing, "market" criteria influence the allocation of a reduced share of total investment funds.

Efficiency Handicaps

A brief description was provided in Chapter II of the concept of growth in "potential GNP." As was explained there, this growth is estimated on the basis of labor-force and productivity projections. Productivity, in turn, is calculated in terms of output per unit of labor input and is normally estimated crudely by extrapolating trend lines based on experience over some previous period of time (a decade, say).

This concept of productivity gives the mistaken impression that labor alone contributes to, and is therefore solely responsible for, productivity advances. Many other factors are involved, of course, including especially the rate and type of capital formation, managerial skills, innovation, and technological progress. A better measure of the rate of improvement in an economy's performance is that of "total factor" productivity. For the sake of simplicity, we will refer to this concept as reflecting an economy's "efficiency."

Efficiency is a term widely used but just as widely misunderstood. It refers, in essence, to an economy's success in getting the most out of the least. It is also a concept that can be applied on a broad scale. Thus there is no reason why its use must be constrained to performance in producing physical output. One can quite easily apply this concept to performance in the areas of environmental protection, exploitation of exhaustible mineral resources, and even the use of leisure time.

One of the problems that must be faced in the calculation of efficiency performance is that conventional economic statistics define output very narrowly in terms of goods and services. With changing social preferences, other dimensions of output — environmental quality, working conditions, health levels — will increasingly be incorporated into the concept of output, and this has led to the development of "social indicators." What must be recognized, however, is that people expecting progress on these other fronts should have lower expectations in terms of the rate of increase in material living standards.[5] Thus far the dominant public attitude appears to be one of putting pressure on government to achieve a greater range of goals without volunteering to pay for them — the "free-lunch" syndrome.

It is possible to define output broadly enough so that "slow growth" need not be an inevitable prospect. The inclusion of leisure time as a factor in total well-being, for example, would greatly alter assessments of past and future performance. Handicaps to efficiency, however, lower output-growth potential, no matter how one chooses to define output.

The pursuit of efficiency is a demanding task. It requires discipline, flexibility, mobility, and foresight, among other characteristics. The task is so demanding, in fact, that, as income rises, people are likely to strive for efficiency with progressively less vigor, sacrificing a portion of potential further gains for a quieter life. (One way to phrase this is that efficiency is an "inferior" good — implying that consumption in the form of tolerance for inefficiency rises at a faster pace than income.) A weakening of the drive to acquire additional physical goods as income rises cannot be dismissed as irrational. But when a nation's policies reflect such a development, handicaps emerge in the generation of wealth for redistributive transfer programs, an economy's adaptability to change is reduced, and protectionist pressures proliferate.

Many sources of inefficiency arise from imperfections in the operation of markets. These imperfections include barriers to entry that inhibit competition in product and in input (for example, labor) markets, discriminatory behavior, and "externalities" — costs or benefits that are not fully charged or are not credited to those causing or earning them. Many commentators would equate structural problems with imperfections in markets. Some (for example, John Kenneth

---

[5] This discussion raises one of the most perplexing problems currently facing industrial democracies. On the one hand, interest groups proliferate and demand policy actions whose costs are only partially borne by their members. On the other hand, whereas some individuals would voluntarily pay for the achievement of non-materialistic objectives, policies to achieve these objectives often impact on those who would not agree to pay voluntarily. For example, strict environmental standards may make certain industries uncompetitive internationally, leading to job losses for those poorly trained or unsuitably located for alternative employment.

Galbraith) would go much further and attribute inflation largely to these imperfections. This line of argument underlies the prescription that permanent controls must be placed upon "big business" and "big labor."

There is very little empirical support for the contention that markets have become more dominated by large concentrations of private power (corporate or union) than they were in the past. What does appear to be happening is that the actions of large corporations and labor unions limit the potential for actual declines in prices and wages during periods of economic slack. Moreover, strong pressures have emerged — and not only among large corporations and labor unions — to pass inflation forward or backward to others, thereby complicating the process of bringing inflation under control quickly. Thus we see another set of rigidities of the sort discussed earlier, resulting in an inflationary bias in contemporary industrial economies.

An area where some of the greatest handicaps to efficiency have emerged in recent years is government intervention, which requires a chapter of its own. Before turning to the expanding role of government, the following conclusions serve to summarize this chapter.

- Institutional and attitudinal rigidities are frustrating the process of adjusting to the underlying causes of inflation in modern industrial societies. These rigidities are deeply entrenched and are unlikely to be eliminated quickly or easily. The contribution to the solution of these problems from the strategy of gradualism is limited. Slack economic conditions may reduce resistance to necessary adjustments, but that result is uncertain and may only be temporary.

- The burden of adjustment appears to be falling disproportionately on the side of output-expanding investment. Slow growth in investment demand may be camouflaging the true extent of excess demand on the world's output potential and of residual inflationary pressures remaining in the system. The longer such slow growth persists, the greater will be the difficulties experienced in finding the path back to full employment with price stability.

- Society's views on efficiency appear to be changing. In part this is the result of changing social goals. In addition, forces appear to be operating to blunt the drive for efficiency; to the extent this is true, there are negative consequences in terms of meeting economic- and social-policy targets.

- The entire economy suffers to the extent that its growth is restrained below potential as part of an anti-inflation strategy. The rigidities described in this section make it difficult to figure out the allocation of these costs of inflation as it is currently being experienced. As a result of these complications, traditional theories about how reductions in inflationary pressures will come about are suspect.

- The most serious costs of inflation are likely to be observed in the dynamic performance of an economy. As disequilibrium conditions persist, they have a tendency to accumulate and feed on themselves, embedding more deeply a set of problems that were initially of a short-term nature.

V. The Role of Government: Intervention and Disincentives

Topics relating to the role of government have been touched upon at various points in this monograph. In this chapter the different themes and strands are brought together in a somewhat more systematic manner. Three topics are treated: growth in the size of government; the direct impact of government sector growth on the inflation process; and contributions to the inflation-unemployment problem.

This section is not intended to be a blanket indictment of government. Such an approach is unjustified and inappropriate. Government participation or intervention in the economic affairs of modern societies cannot be evaluated effectively in terms of simple or one-sided explanations. In large measure, governments are bigger and more active because of the problems that confront modern society and because the public persists in demanding more of, and from, them. Other factors are also involved: the ease of access to means of financing government growth; the unwillingness of political leaders to say "no" to uneconomic or excessive demands; the evolution of bureaucratic expertise in finding new tasks to perform; the separation of the political from the bureaucratic control of decision-making processes; duplicative functions performed at different levels of government; and the tendency for government to think it has a responsibility to tackle, on behalf of the public, age-old problems that may have no solutions.

Government has a number of legitimate and important roles in an economy, not least of which is that of supplying the basic capital and organizational infrastructure needed if an economy is to function effectively. There is a disturbing tendency to move from the accounting convention that attributes very low direct productivity growth to the government sector to the conclusion that all government spending is counterproductive. In fact, an economy's performance should be viewed as a systemic whole, with government making a potentially valuable input to that whole. In recent years, however, government has overreached itself in terms of the public's toleration for paying the bill, and the outcome has been a sharp swing in the direction of the public's perceiving government as inherently wasteful. The following observations attempt to analyze why this situation has developed.

Growth in the Size of Government

Government expenditures in all nations have, to varying degrees, increased absolutely and in relation to the value of total output. For analytical purposes it is necessary to differentiate among four classes of expenditure growth; experience with respect to each class differs widely among nations.

New or Expanded Government Services

Expenditures falling within this class include those for the creation of new government departments (for example, environmental protection, consumer affairs, and energy research) and for the expansion of existing department services (for example, health, education, and defense). The implications of more rapid growth in these kinds of expenditures relative to overall growth have been examined in the writings of Robert Bacon and Walter Eltis.[1]

The Bacon and Eltis thesis, in brief, is that these types of expenditures increase claims on "market" output without increasing the total size of that output. As the ratio of this spending to total spending rises, it is argued, other claims on market output are "crowded out." The result is a reduced growth of exports (and/or increased growth of imports), creating balance of payments problems; reduced output-expanding investment, creating a slower growth potential and unemployment problems; and a reduced proportion of market output available for distribution to producers of that output, creating frustration and inflationary pressures.

There is a serious danger of overstatement of this thesis. The distinction between "market" and "non-market" activity is inherently arbitrary. (For example, increased expenditures on education might be classified as "non-market," but may expand the quality or the quantity of the production potential of the "market" sector in the future.) Furthermore, because a given expenditure fails to add to market output does not mean that it has no value to society. (A cleaner environment resulting from the enforcement of new air or water purity standards would be regarded by many as highly desirable in its own right and could improve the long-term performance of the economy.)

Nevertheless, the Bacon-Eltis thesis is particularly revealing when combined with their reports of numerous instances where government expenditures have increased because of rising inputs of government employees with little or no improvement in output by available objective standards of measurement (for example, the rise in the ratio of administrators per student or per patient in schools and hospitals). Even if output were to increase, there is the fundamental issue of whether the public desires that output as reflected in a willingness to pay voluntarily for its cost.

---

[1] Robert Bacon and Walter Eltis, *Britain's Economic Problem: Too Few Producers*, 2nd ed. (London: The Macmillan Press, 1978).

Replacement of Private Services with Public Services

Government spending will increase if services formerly provided as a private service are supplied as a public service paid for from government revenues (health care and university education would be examples in some countries). Several issues arise from this type of public spending. First, is the service provided at least as efficiently by the public sector as by the private sector? If not, potential output in the economy is reduced. Second, does the method of pricing the service encourage increased consumption of it? (This would be the case for any universal program that bears a charge for use that is below the incremental cost of service, such as heavily subsidized medical care.) Programs of this sort distort decisions regarding resource allocation and encourage the notion that government services are a "free good." Third, do these programs involve an element of income redistribution, intentionally or unintentionally? If so (and they do in the majority of cases), the impacts are the same as with redistributive transfer payments, discussed below.

Replacement of Private Ownership with Public Ownership

Increased public ownership of enterprises through nationalization raises government's share of economic activity. The efficiency issue emerges again here. Another issue is the price paid for nationalized assets, which may or may not be at "fair market value." If it is not, wealth redistribution is involved. Many government-owned enterprises are directly or indirectly subsidized, which raises issues similar to those when government services are provided at prices below incremental costs to the economy.

Redistributive Transfer Payments

In the vast majority of countries this type of activity has been responsible for the most significant proportion of increased government spending. Costs of administering such programs raise issues that are essentially the same as when new or expanded government services are undertaken. The transfers themselves do not use up an economy's resources, but they may shift income from those with relatively higher savings preferences to those with relatively lower savings preferences, adding to inflationary pressures in a period of demand excesses.

In addition to these four categories of spending, there are two other types of government activity that influence an economy's performance but involve no, or very limited, direct expenditures.

Tax Concessions

As an alternative to direct subsidies (which would show up under the first category of spending above), governments can accomplish essentially the same results through tax concessions — the equivalent of an expenditure of a tax revenue. These concessions invariably influence the allocation of resources within an economy, but there is no way to determine the inherent desirability of their impact. Given a particular social goal, the most one can say is that a particular method for meeting that goal is or is not the most efficient possible. What can be argued, however, is that special treatment of the recipients of tax concessions (or subsidies) means they become beholden to government for the continuation of that treatment.

Regulation

Regulation of market activities may take a variety of forms, from the establishment of rules for sale or purchase, to the determination of ceiling prices, to the imposition of tariffs, quotas, or other barriers to trade. The issues involved in regulation include those already raised in this section plus others too numerous to list here. The main point is that regulatory activity is a central feature of the role of government in modern economic activity; and while the traditional justification for regulation is to correct market distortions, regulatory activities may introduce their own distortions, with the increase in spending for the administration of regulations being only a portion of the overall impact.

Direct Impact of Government Sector Growth on the Inflation Process

The first class of government spending described in the preceding section (new or expanded services) tends to contribute most directly to excess-demand inflation. The other classes involve much more complicated reasoning and measurement before such a conclusion can be drawn. The second and third classes (involving shifts of existing activities from the private to the public sector) include an especially complex set of analytical problems and will receive little attention here. In the fourth class (redistributive transfers), however, there are problems in common with the first class with respect to "tax-push" (a variant of "cost-push") inflation. These two classes are often treated as very different for analytical purposes, but they should not be when the subject is inflation other than of the excess-demand variety.

Government spending, whether for services or for transfer payments, must be financed. The emphasis in this discussion will be on financing through tax revenues, although deficit financing produces similar final results through a different, and more circuitous, reasoning. Taxes are a cost, and resistance to paying the cost contributes directly to the inflation process. This resistance can take a number of forms. Income earners may demand monetary adjustments tied to cost-of-living indices. Higher indirect taxes (for example, sales taxes) show up quickly in price indices and are automatically passed on to those paying incomes indexed to these indices. Direct taxes on wages (for example, personal income and payroll taxes) will show up in bargaining demands if workers base these demands on after-tax incomes. And direct taxes on capital (for example, the corporate income tax) will, unless profits are abnormally high, eventually show up in higher prices and higher rates of price inflation, which eventually show up in higher indexed incomes.

It might be argued that a stable tax will not give rise to inflationary pressures. Furthermore, with a stable but progressive personal-income-tax structure, government expenditure can rise more rapidly than total income without requiring increased borrowing. It is not clear whether income earners are resistant to accepting the consequences of a progressive tax system when prices are reasonably stable. Logic would suggest they would be more so, the steeper is the rate of progression. Resistance is likely to be much higher, however, in a period of inflation, when pay increases to reflect inflation move the taxpayer through progressively higher incremental tax steps. In recognition of the above problem, Canada introduced measures to index, at the federal level (followed by all provinces except Quebec), personal income taxes by adjusting certain deductions and tax brackets for inflation.

The key point here is that taxpayers appear to be resisting paying for increased government spending on new programs and on transfers that have expanded more rapidly than national income. In part this resistance is institutionalized in COLAs; a revolt against higher government spending is also seen in such voter responses as those to Proposition 13 in California.

Contributions to the Inflation-Unemployment Problem

Increased government spending in at least the first three categories mentioned earlier means that more and more workers are bargaining with government as employer. The main problem this raises is that government brings no direct market discipline to bear on these negotiations. Furthermore, in many of its negotiations government is under public pressure to settle without a work stoppage; and if it fails there are political costs to bear. Finally, productivity measures are often difficult to devise for services, especially government services. This deprives government negotiators of a benchmark commonly used in private sector negotiations.

A probable complicating factor in public sector wage negotiations is that public sector employees have changed their attitudes toward wages vis-à-vis job security. In an era when unemployment was a much more serious risk and the burdens of being unemployed more severe, the higher security associated with government employment translated into a greater tolerance for relatively lower wages in that sector. In recent years, however, with security being less of a perceived benefit, public sector employees have been seeking to "catch up" not only with inflation, but with wages for comparable jobs in the private sector. This process is creating tensions in both sectors: private sector employees react to the perception of a less demanding work environment, to greater job security, and — in many countries — to favorable fringe benefits (especially pensions) in the public service; public service employees react to take-home-pay differentials in comparison with the private sector. (Instances of public sector remuneration exceeding private sector remuneration have been increasing in some countries in recent years.)

In its search for greater social equity, government has created, often unintentionally, serious distortions in economic performance in the form of disincentives. The search for greater equity without these disincentives has been a difficult one, and there is a tendency to overstate the magnitude of the problem (for example, the notion that the majority of welfare recipients are lazy but able-bodied workers). Still, there has been more than a marginal impact from disincentives on economic efficiency; even if this were not the case, perceptions are important.

A Concluding Observation

The most significant effect of the increase in the size of government may well lie in its aggregate impact on traditional individualistic values such as discipline, self-reliance, and initiative. The larger government becomes and the more accustomed individuals, groups, and firms are to looking to it to provide answers to their economic problems, the more likely these problems will become magnified. If government has the responsibility of keeping unemployment down, why worry about competitiveness? If government can be relied upon to protect and subsidize troubled industries and regions, why not adopt the quiet life, which is so much more relaxing than the competitive struggle? And if every demand expressed loudly enough receives a hearing and generates a response, why moderate these demands?

The hypothesis might be advanced, although there is probably no way to test it rigorously, that an economy's performance is a function of how it is "managed." The greater the complexity of "management" (that is, interference), the lower appears to be its relative performance, subject to historical factors that may generate tolerance for management in pursuit of shared national goals. If there is any validity to this hypothesis, slower growth, which economists are trying to explain with all manner of "structural" rationalizations, may be a result of the fact that modern industrial societies have become reluctant to risk the instabilities, the burdens, and the disciplines of the "unmanaged" market and have increasingly turned over the responsibilities formerly associated with individualism to governments no longer able to cope with the magnitude of tasks they have been too willing to take on.

What is really at issue here is the future of "mixed-enterprise" economic systems. Few would deny that both the private and the public sectors have effective roles to play in modern industrial democracies. There may well be, however, a critical mass beyond which the overall influence of government cannot go without turning a "mixed" system into a "fixed" system. If that critical mass has been reached, debates about the strategy of gradualism are likely to turn out to be quite sterile.

VI. Pragmatic Policy Responses

Despite confident assurances by various government officials to the contrary, as of late 1978 there were few clear signs of sustained progress toward a return of balanced conditions in the world economy. Unemployment remained high and was still climbing in many countries. Inflation rates had subsided from their earlier peaks, but price rises, especially in the United States, had again become a serious policy concern. Government deficits were at exceptionally high levels, and very large imbalances continued to be a characteristic of the international payments positions of key nations. This environment fostered widespread anxiety, frustration, and defeatism.

There are ways out of the current common economic predicament. Pragmatic policy responses, however, must be tailored to the specific problems and circumstances facing individual nations. Moreover, while a return to the economic fundamentals associated with discipline is a necessary condition for success, it is not a sufficient condition. Inflation is, at its foundation, a social malady and must ultimately be attacked at a socio-political level. There is no more serious challenge to the future of democratic nations in the industrial world than the determined launching of this attack.

This concluding chapter is divided into three sections. The first reviews some of the primary lessons to be drawn from recent experience and thus provides some general guidelines for designing a basic policy strategy. The second contains a brief analysis of several alternatives to gradualism. The conclusion reached is that the most promising option is likely to be a set of revisions to the gradualist approach, supplemented by a major campaign to deal with structural rigidities. In the final section several observations are made about actions that could be taken to improve public understanding of the trade-offs involved as nations attempt to improve their longer-term economic performances.

Designing a Strategy: Clear Lessons from the Recent Past

A fundamental premise of this monograph is that there is no simple solution to the inflation-unemployment problem. Arguments to the contrary serve only to confuse the policy-making process and to misinform the public about the nature of the challenges to be met. Defeatism, however, is inappropriate. The point from which to begin framing a constructive strategy is the recognition of certain lessons that stand out from a survey of economic events over the past several years. These reflect reasoned observations of recent history rather than any dogmatic interpretation aimed at proving the validity of a particular economic philosophy.

- The growth rate of the money supply is, over time, the single most important determinant of the inflation rate. A government seeking to promote price stability must keep the money supply from growing rapidly over a prolonged period.
- Rapid increases in the share of total spending accounted for by government tend to generate inflationary pressures. New long-term spending programs should not be undertaken as a means of offsetting cyclical downturns in the economy; such new programs should reflect public awareness and discussion of the long-term consequences for revenue (taxation) requirements.
- Although specific instances of governmental intervention in economic affairs might be justified as reasonable and in the public interest, the sum total of these interventions may well have a "critical mass" effect that alters the very foundations of an economy's incentive system with unintended, and unpredictable, consequences. Abdication to government of individual responsibilities has become a deceptively easy option in the face of increasingly complex societal problems; reasoned resistance to excessive intervention by government is a measure of a nation's democratic vitality.
- Rigidity in the standards against which economic performance is assessed is inappropriate in a period of significant structural changes, such as major shifts in national demographic profiles or in the relative costs of basic commodities such as energy. The goal of "full" employment, for example, should not be viewed in relation to a single percentage of the labor force that is invariant over time.
- Effective policies must be geared to a number of performance goals, and the guiding principle should be to do better on each over time, even if that means sacrificing, at a point in time, the best possible performance with respect to any one goal.
- Economic forecasting is an art, not an exact science; the correct dosage of corrective policy measures is difficult to calculate; and there are long lags in the process of converting policy advice into policy action. Steadiness in the application of sound policies is therefore likely to prove superior over time to continuous exercises in *ad hoc* "fine tuning."
- In policy initiatives the supply side of the economic equation should receive at least as much emphasis as the demand side. Strong growth performance depends upon adequate capital formation; the provision of managerial skills; people trained for, and willing to work in, the jobs that are available; constant improvements in technology; and a societal environment that encourages efficiency, adaptability, and entrepreneurship. The increased handicaps to growth described in earlier chapters add to the importance of supply-oriented policy measures.

- Flexible exchange rates cure some problems and create others; they are not an all-purpose corrective. Some developments — such as the oil-price increase of 1973-74, prolonged periods of significant variations in national inflation rates, and marked differences in productivity performances over time — may require that established exchange-rate relationships be abandoned. But abandonment of a rigid rate pattern in the face of fundamental changes in the determinants of relative currency values is quite different from abandoning the target of restoring reasonable stability in rates. Expectations that governments will pursue policies to achieve such stability represent an important discipline in economic affairs, and these expectations should not be discarded.

These lessons provide guidelines for a policy strategy that would help nations achieve a more balanced economic performance and maintain that performance over time within acceptable limits of inflation and unemployment. They also provide criteria against which to judge policies aimed at correcting a situation in which performance has been allowed to depart significantly from these limits.

Gradualism and Its Alternatives

The primary reason many nations have gravitated toward gradualism is that there appears to be no other alternative that has a high probability of working without exposing governments to very high political risks. Two major alternatives have been contemplated, and in some cases implemented, but the results in theory or in practice are, at best, mixed.

The "Crunch" Approach

One alternative is to tolerate, or even provoke, a sharp recession, thereby generating sufficient slack in the economy to deflate inflationary pressures. This strategy, which might be called the "crunch" approach, has the appeal that, if it is applied quickly and firmly enough in an emerging inflationary environment, it should prevent inflationary expectations from becoming deeply embedded within the economy. The necessary slowdown, although fairly severe in the short run, can probably be of relatively short duration, at least in theory. A major weakness of the gradualist strategy has been that unemployment remains moderately high over a prolonged period; it is quite possible that the resulting cumulative loss in output will be greater than if the crunch had been applied.

Virtually all governments in the industrialized world accepted a recession and a rise in unemployment immediately following the surge in world oil prices in late 1973 and early 1974. But this experience fell short of a real crunch, and the inflationary spiral was not broken. There are many reasons why success in curbing inflation proved so limited, with the major ones being as follows:

- The crunch approach is a politically viable strategy only if it is adopted relatively early in a government's term in office. The closer a nation is to an election, the greater the pressures within the political process to stimulate growth in order to show the voters an improved growth and unemployment performance. (Growth stimulus reduces unemployment more quickly than it rekindles price increases.)

- As a consequence of more generous income-maintenance programs for the unemployed, a great deal of unemployment appears to be needed to produce a significant moderation in wage demands. Few governments are prepared to accept that much slack in the face of adverse public reaction.

- Unless most nations pursue the crunch approach at the same time, international pressures mount to ease up on the few that do, possibly prematurely for their domestic objectives. (These pressures have been felt by West Germany and Japan in recent years.) Moreover, those same nations tend, in a flexible-exchange-rate system, to experience revaluations of their currencies, which in turn tend to shift the distribution of income away from profits, especially in export-oriented industries. The result is a decline in the incentive to invest.

- It is by no means clear that a crunch approach is superior to any other in bringing about a permanent downward adjustment in income demands. Inflation will persist if a return to more rapid growth is seen as an opportunity to make up for ground lost during the crunch — the catch-up syndrome.

Given the level of unemployment that exists in the industrialized world, a general move to the crunch approach now would run a very high risk of causing a depression. This alternative to gradualism, therefore, can appeal at this time only to those who might argue that inflation has become so serious a problem that this risk must be taken. Such a pessimistic conclusion does not, in our view, seem warranted.

Income Controls

A second alternative — some would say a necessary supplement — to gradualism is to try to deal with inflation by resorting to some form of income controls. The historical record indicates that controls have had, at best, only a minor impact on inflation over time; that record is one of the main reasons why a strong majority of economists would argue against their use. Most economists contend that it is better for a nation to practice restraint in the creation of money and in government spending, thereby dealing with the causes, rather than the symptoms, of inflation.

A case can be made for controls, but only under a special set of conditions. If expectations that inflation will persist have become deeply embedded in an economy and if the government has become firmly committed to conducting policy in line with the lessons mentioned earlier, then controls may assist in easing the transition to a more balanced economic performance. Specifically, it can be argued that controls would permit officials to reduce inflation while allowing more rapid growth, and thus less unemployment, than would be possible without controls. In short, controls might provide a "breathing space" during which more disciplined policies could be allowed to work.

The weakness in this line of reasoning lies in the tendency of governments to waste breathing spaces. Controls seem to have the effect of lulling officials into believing that difficult policy initiatives can be approached at a relaxed pace. But the time during which controls have a chance of being effective is limited, and this relaxation of pressures on policy-makers may work against the original purpose of controls.

Up to this point we have referred to temporary controls. Some commentators — notably John Kenneth Galbraith — advocate permanent controls on a selective basis. Their reasoning is that certain sectors of an industrialized economy are largely immune to anti-inflation policies applied at a general level. It is argued that those sectors characterized by large corporations and large unions can pass along higher wages via higher prices with relative impunity because of an absence of effective competitive forces. Rather than debate at length the validity of this characterization of the modern economy, we simply note that this comes down to a concern about the structural nature of the inflation problem, which we have argued is one thing not dealt with effectively in the gradualist strategy as it has been employed to date.

Refinements to Gradualism

The conclusion we reach is that gradualism is the most pragmatic strategy for trying to resolve the current international economic predicament. When comparing gradualism in practice with the lessons outlined in the preceding section, however, we note that some important gaps remain to be filled with concrete policy initiatives. Attention must now be turned to lessons concerning the supply side of the economic equation and the almost exclusive reliance upon exchange-rate flexibility to sort out international payments imbalances.

It has become the conventional wisdom to blame inflation on people collectively "living beyond their means." The common prescription is that people should lower their income expectations. While it is imperative that expectations be kept in line with potentials, an economy's potential is a variable. In other words, a supplementary prescription is to increase the "means" at a society's disposal.

It is possible to expand potential by devising policies that would:

- increase the share of national output devoted to productive capital formation. Capital should be defined broadly to include the acquisition of skills by the labor force, the development of a greater capacity to generate output without imposing excessive long-term costs on the physical environment, and the accumulation of more plants and machines.
- encourage research and development activities and, probably more important, the speedier diffusion of new technology throughout an economy.
- improve the process whereby an economy responds to changing circumstances by providing incentives to adjust to change rather than to resist it.

Structural problems essentially boil down to constraints on potential supply growth. Because these problems are politically difficult to address, and have become more so as they have increased in number and significance, the short-term reaction has been to try to protect and isolate from competitive forces those sectors under the most intense challenge. The longer-term consequence of such a reaction is to hold down potential growth and to aggravate inflationary pressures and unemployment.

An essential component of a set of supply-oriented policies is an environment conducive to growth; stagnation in demand does not constitute such an environment. This is where the problem of international payments imbalances enters the picture.

Concern over the risks of increasing inflationary pressures by stimulating growth has been carried too far. A further rise in unemployment, which is a definite near-term prospect in many developed nations, would result in very little inflation relief in most countries. (The United States, which has experienced a sharp decline in unemployment since 1976, may be an exception, given inflationary pressures that appear to be rebuilding there.) But additional slack would make it more difficult to control the trend toward increased protectionism in trade relations and otherwise make less likely a prompt response to structural problems. It would also discourage increased capital formation.

Nations with balance of payments deficits, however, have become constrained in their ability to act alone in stimulating demand. Such stimulus would tend to weaken further the payments position because imports would increase while exports would not. The result would be more downward pressure on the currency, with inflationary consequences.

It is therefore the responsibility of nations with strong balance of payments positions to lead a general, but moderate and steady, expansion of demand on a global scale. This stimulus, in turn, would be more consistent with long-term needs if it were focused on incentives to expand output potential rather than on direct encouragement of additional current consumption (public or private). If successful, supply incentives will quickly translate into increased consumption as payments are made to factors of production employed in supply-expanding activities. These payments will also provide an expanding tax base that should eventually more than offset the temporarily higher government deficits that stimulative measures will require.

The term "supply expansion" covers a very broad range of policy options. Few specific recommendations along these lines would be appropriate for all countries. The important point is that the supply side will require the greatest emphasis if the strategy of gradualism is to be brought to a successful conclusion. A fatalistic acceptance of the notion that rigid limits to growth have suddenly eliminated the viability of this approach is neither appropriate nor logical.

The Importance of Reason

To conclude this monograph, we turn from the pragmatic to the philosophic. Nothing is inevitable in economic affairs, and economic logic alone will not determine the course along which democratic societies proceed. The solution to the collective economic predicament lies in creating and maintaining a social environment in which the rule of reason is fostered and basic facts are communicated objectively and received and acted upon in a spirit of accommodation and with understanding of the predicament. That the predicament is serious has become increasingly obvious; the challenge facing governments is to mobilize the concern that now exists in order to achieve realistic and enlightened goals.

Nations in the industrialized world are searching for effective mechanisms to better reconcile expectations and potentials. Historically, periodic slumps in economic activity were relied upon to achieve that reconciliation. However, that option has lost much of its effectiveness as income-maintenance programs for the unemployed have been improved and as elected governments have come to be judged largely on their ability to avoid sharp economic downturns. In this situation, efforts by individuals and organized groups to promote their maximum self-interest have been carried on without the overall discipline necessary to ensure a general balance in national economic performances.

The search for new reconciliation mechanisms has led to experiments in consultative processes in which business, labor, and other groups meet with government officials in pursuit of shared understanding of problems and solutions. These experiments have varied widely in form among countries. In some cases the process has been formalized in legislation; in others the approach is very informal. Mechanics are as different as the historical, political, and cultural backgrounds of the nations attempting this approach. The common feature of these experiments is the attempt to provide a framework within which the pursuit of group interests can be channeled and constrained in order to ensure long-term national viability. It is the willingness to sacrifice some short-term group interests for long-term collective goals that measures the health and vitality of any social organization.

New forms of consultative mechanisms can serve a valuable purpose in complex modern economies. To be effective, however, these mechanisms must be based upon two-way, interactive flows of information. In one direction, objective, professional, and relevant information concerning policy options, constraints, and consequences must flow to the general public. If this is to lead to a more knowledgeable electorate, however, the public-education system must produce school-leavers with a far better grasp than they have today of economic trade-offs, cause-and-effect relationships, and the illusory nature of "free lunches" promised by office-seekers.

It is also important that the primary conveyors of information to the general public — the media — take a more responsible attitude toward subjects they have traditionally regarded as either too arcane or too dull to merit much time or space. Reporters must be given more opportunity to achieve a degree of mastery of the policy topics they cover by being allowed and encouraged to specialize, and the commentators selected for exposure by the media must be chosen more for their reason and insight than for their ability to popularize and to titilate or for the aggressiveness with which they propound particular doctrines.

The other essential flow of information is from the private sector to political leaders, in order that the policy-making process can better reflect the practical consequences of various policy options. The bureaucratization of the decision-making process has, to a significant extent, resulted from a crowding-out of the discretionary time that political leaders have at their disposal. Far too often, political leaders view participation in consultative processes as an obligation. The exercise of good political judgment will always be an essential part of sound policy formation, so political leaders must come to a consultative forum as people with time to listen, respond, reflect, and then act.

The main danger of consultative mechansims is that they will become an additional forum for the fighting-out of new power relationships, while those groups excluded from the consultations seek out alternative channels for promoting their points of view. This process would, in all likelihood, raise, rather than subdue, the aggressiveness with which policy issues are debated.

In response to this danger, it would be helpful if political parties could reach an agreement that some economic issues and goals are basically non-partisan in nature. The primary economic goals outlined in Chapter II, for example, are shared by the major parties in each country. So too are certain perceptions (along the lines of the lessons described earlier in this chapter) about the appropriate policy strategy to follow. Even if agreement were to be reached at these levels, thereby depoliticizing economic debates somewhat, there would still be plenty of room for differences in party positions to be aired on questions regarding priorities and trade-offs.

The issue comes down, in the end, to the challenge of how to reinvigorate the process of responsible democracy within nations whose economic problems seem so complex and numerous that defeatism has become widespread. The place to begin is with a manageable list of topics for which public participation in an effective consultative process has a reasonable chance of producing meaningful results. Two candidates for that list conclude this discussion.

- It should be possible to reach some agreement on the amount of inflation that can be compensated for on a general, across-the-board basis. As explained at various points in this monograph, that amount will be less than the full rise in the consumer (retail) price index because of a need to make basic adjustments in living styles to reflect such factors as higher energy costs. These adjustments should be widely shared on an equitable basis. Agreement could (and should) also be sought regarding those individuals or groups (for example, pension recipients) who should receive a more generous inflation adjustment in pursuit of a "fair" sharing of output.

- Some broader understanding should also be possible concerning the issue of capital formation, which we have argued lies at the heart of supply-side approaches to the inflation-unemployment problem. There is a tendency to regard policies to boost investment as being designed primarily to shift income to the more well-to-do in a society. A better information base and greater appreciation by the public of the actual distribution of claims on the output of capital investment are essential. So is a careful analysis of policy options that would increase productive capital formation as a share of GNP without generating a major redistribution of future income flows. One possibility, for example, would be tax policies to encourage the flow of individuals' savings into direct-ownership or equity claims on productive enterprises.

Inflation is a social malady. The cure will not be found in simple economic prescriptions or in the treatment of symptoms, but in reasoned responses by society as a whole through a commitment to long-term objectives compatible with the maintenance of individual freedoms.

Appendix

A Summary and Critique of the McCracken Report

Gennifer Sussman*

The report formally titled *Towards Full Employment and Price Stability* was prepared for the Organisation for Economic Co-operation and Development by Paul McCracken and a group of independent experts and was released in mid-1977.[1] The terms of reference for the group were to "identify and consider the main policy issues involved in the pursuit, by member countries, of non-inflationary economic growth and high employment levels in the light of the structural changes which have taken place in the recent past" and to suggest strategies and instruments that could be adopted by members at national and international levels in order to deal with these issues. The group felt that "the whole cluster of economic, political, social, and moral issues associated with the relationships between developed and developing nations" fell outside the scope of the study. The report focuses on better management of the market-oriented economies of the industrialized democracies.[2] The central theme is the importance of the industrial economies' finding the "narrow path" back toward full employment and price stability on the basis of the group's reading of the causes of present problems and the lessons of the past. The discussion is mainly at a general level, with limited analysis of the particular problems of individual countries. Little space is given to the "international dimension," and the discussion of this aspect of current problems is superficial.[3]

The group's reading of recent economic history is that although there have been underlying changes in behavior patterns and power relationships internationally and within countries, "the most important feature was an unusual bunching of unfortunate disturbances unlikely to be repeated on the same scale, the impact of which was compounded by some avoidable errors in economic policy" (p. 103). The report seeks to answer three fundamental questions: "What went wrong and why? What are the objectives of, and constraints on, policies over the next ten years or so? What are the broad policy options open to us?" (p. 11)

What Went Wrong and Why? The Origins of Present Problems

Excess demand arose in the United States during the Viet Nam war. A wage-price explosion toward the end of the 1960s was followed by restrictive policies and the downturn of 1970-71. U.S. deficits, loss of confidence in the dollar, and rapid increases in liquidity elsewhere led to a breakdown of the fixed-exchange-rate system.

---

*Staff Economist, C. D. Howe Research Institute.

[1] Organisation for Economic Co-operation and Development, Paris, June, 1977. Members of the group are listed at the end of this appendix. Page references throughout this appendix refer to the report.

[2] The analysis concentrates on a representative group of member countries, including all the larger OECD economies — United States, Japan, Germany, France, United Kingdom, Italy, and Canada — together with the Netherlands and Sweden to include the experience of two smaller, very open economies. These nine countries account for seven-eighths of the total output of the twenty-four OECD member countries (p. 44).

[3] This weakness is referred to in comments by individual members (pp. 247-55).

Appendix

Subsequently, overly expansionary policies in 1972-73, particularly monetary expansion in the absence of balance of payments constraints, caused a speculative boom. Bottlenecks appeared because of the rapid increase in demand. The oil crisis came when economies were already turning downward because of restrictive policies introduced earlier in 1973, which were continued because there were few alternatives given speculative behavior and a new wage-price spiral. The recovery that began in the middle of 1975 is fragile. It is striking, the report notes, that although inflation rates have dropped, they are highly divergent.

The Lessons of the Past

The key to the group's analysis is its assessment that a combination of shocks and policy errors were the principal causes of the current economic predicament of the industrial economies. Out of this arises its conviction that the deteriorating trade-off between output and inflation can be improved by demand management. "This does not mean that demand management is no longer effective in reducing inflation. We reject the view that existing market-oriented economic systems and democratic political institutions have failed. What is needed is better use of existing instruments of economic policy, and better functioning and management of existing market mechanisms" (p. 14 — see also pp. 103-04).

Three types of factors are noted as contributing to worsening performance in industrial economies.

Shocks

The food and oil price explosions and the breakdown of pegged exchange rates have produced adjustment problems that have generated shocks internationally.

Policy Errors

Macro-policy shifts contributed to wider fluctuations — they tended to be too late, too long, or of the wrong size. The major error was overly expansionary policy (especially monetary) at the beginning of the 1970s. "We do not think it debatable that the massive increase in monetary aggregates beginning in 1970 contributed significantly to the excessive speed of the 1972-73 boom, the buildup of inflationary pressures, and stubborn inflationary expectations" (p. 102).

Changes in Basic Relationships Within the Economic System

Part of the worsening performance must be attributed to more fundamental factors that are less easy to deal with:

- The maturing of the postwar generation, which may have contributed to "altered views and changing values" as well as to "growing unrest in labour markets."
- The increasing economic and political power of the developing countries. Growing concern for raw-materials supplies, for example, contributed to sharply increased commodity prices and to the prospect of continually increasing resource costs in the future.
- The increasing public emphasis on income distribution and on the welfare of the populations of developed countries, which has changed economic goals and led to pressures for increased state intervention and administrative control in economic affairs.

- The increasing international interdependence (linkages) and conjunctural developments, which make the system harder to manage and are probably to a large extent irreversible (pp. 102-03).

Having listed these structural factors, the report proceeds to downplay them, going directly to the conclusion that the most important feature of these factors underlying recent experience "was an unusual bunching of unfortunate events unlikely to be repeated on the same scale, the impact of which was compounded by some avoidable errors in economic policy" (p. 103).

The report stresses that, although the 1972-73 boom was closely synchronized in all nine countries in the reference group, so was the 1968 expansion. Levels of resource utilization were also high in both periods. The difference lay in the speed of the expansion.[4] The 1972-73 boom led to an inflationary outburst because of its rapidity, because it was fueled by expansionary monetary policy, and because it also coincided with "some unfortunate accidents." Inflation re-emerged when margins of capacity were still ample, owing to a combination of the speed-limit problem and the accident of rising food prices.[5]

Big price inceases occurred in markets with inelastic supplies that are havens for hedge and speculative funds — real estate and gold, for example — and in the housing market. Overall capacity utilization was not higher than at previous peaks, "but there was an exceptional imbalance between basic materials and advanced processing industries." Low inventories, coupled with inflationary expectations, brought on a scramble for supplies that aggravated shortages. The worldwide commodity boom was the most spectacular symptom of the exceptionally rapid, internationally linked upswing. In 1972-74, prices of foreign-trade goods provided a major impetus to the acceleration of domestic inflation.[6]

Underlying Assumptions: The Trade-Off Between "Activity" and Inflation

The basic assumption the group makes in prescribing policy concerns the short-run trade-off between "activity" and inflation. The report finds that this trade-off has worsened whether measured by the "discomfort index,"[7] as shown in Table 1, or by the relationship between the GDP price deflator and the GDP gap, illustrated in Chart 1.

Toward the end of the 1960s, Phillips curves in the major OECD countries moved outward — that is, a given increase in the CPI (or the wage level) was possible only at progressively higher rates of unemployment. Chart 1[8] illustrates "the way in

---

[4] Between the first halves of 1972 and 1973, real GNP in all OECD countries rose 7½ percent, and industrial production increased 10 percent (p. 58).

[5] Although the report refers to the re-emergence of inflation, the data show a rather steady increase in the aggregate consumer price index of the seven major countries, beginning in 1959.

[6] In earlier expansions, prices of foreign-trade goods rose less than domestic tradeables, which in turn rose less than the GNP deflators. In this period, foreign-trade prices were more sensitive to the rapid increase in demand than were domestic prices (pp. 62 and 107). (This suggests that countries with larger foreign-trade sectors are more susceptible to inflationary pressures in periods of rapidly rising demand.)

[7] The "discomfort index" is the sum of the percentage change in the consumer price index and the unemployment rate.

[8] The "Phillips curve," developed by A. W. Phillips of the London School of Economics, indicated a trade-off between wage-rate changes and the rate of unemployment and was soon generalized to show an inverse relationship between inflation and unemployment. The usefulness of the Phillips curve concept has been questioned in the light of recent experience when

TABLE 1

"Discomfort Index,"
Seven Major Countries, 1959-76

Year	(1) Unemployment Rate (%)	(2) Increase in Consumer Prices (%)	Discomfort Index (1 + 2)
1959	3.8	1.2	5.0
1960	3.4	1.7	5.1
1961	3.6	1.6	5.2
1962	3.1	2.1	5.2
1963	3.2	2.3	5.5
1964	2.9	2.0	4.9
1965	2.7	2.6	5.3
1966	2.5	3.2	5.7
1967	2.8	2.8	5.6
1968	2.7	4.0	6.7
1969	2.6	4.9	7.5
1970	3.1	5.6	8.7
1971	3.7	5.0	8.7
1972	3.7	4.4	8.1
1973	3.2	7.7	10.9
1974	3.7	13.4	17.1
1975	5.4	11.1	16.5
1976	5.3	8.1	13.4
1980 [a]	4.0	5.0	9.0

Note: The "discomfort index" represents a shorthand technique which highlights, in terms of the central dilemma facing economic policy-makers, the deterioration of economic performance in recent years. It is, of course, a crude indicator. By taking an average of the major countries, it ignores problems of international comparability. By concentrating on two variables only, it leaves many aspects of economic — let alone social — performance out of account and, by attributing the same weight to the two variables, begs questions as to the relative extent to which inflation and unemployment in fact create "discomfort." While these reservations would rule out the index for serious analysis, for present purposes the message that emerges seems clear enough.

[a] Estimates taken from "A Growth Scenario to 1980," *OECD Economic Outlook*, No. 19, July, 1976.

Source: Organisation for Economic Co-operation and Development, *Towards Full Employment and Price Stability* (Paris, 1977), p. 42.

CHART 1

**Inflation and Unused Capacity,
Seven Major OECD Countries, 1961-76**

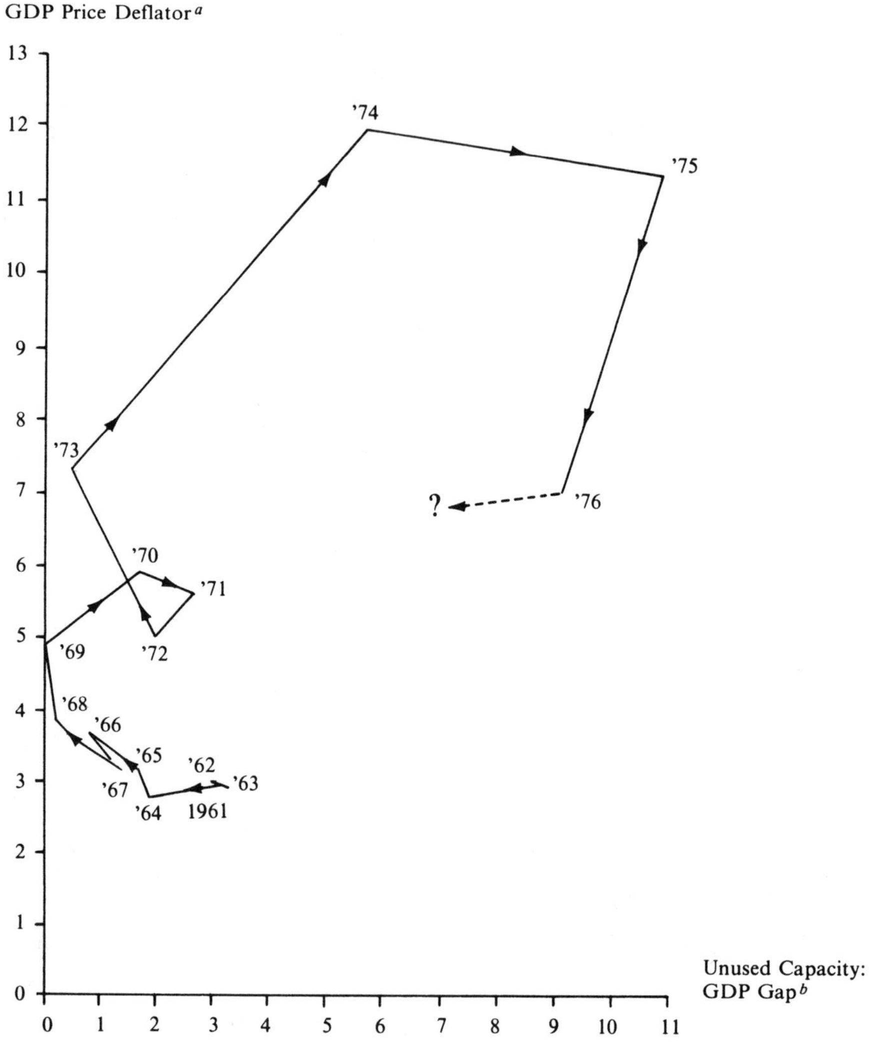

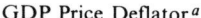

[a] Annual percentage change.
[b] Percentage of potential.

Source: Reproduced from Organisation for Economic Co-operation and Development, *Towards Full Employment and Price Stability* (Paris, 1977), p. 105.

Appendix

which price increases departed explosively from the relationship between unemployment and inflation which prevailed through the 1960s" (p. 104). This shift was caused by a growing confidence in the ability of government to ensure full employment, a declining fear of unemployment and insolvency, and more aggressive income bargaining. So the shocks of 1972-74 took place when Phillips curves both had moved to a less favorable position and were unstable. In the 1970s, however, a major change has occurred in the nature of the short-run trade-off. Inflation no longer originates so much in labor markets, but more in product markets.

The Resulting Conclusions

Agreement on two major conclusions drawn from this analysis forms the basis for the general thrust of the report's policy recommendations. First, deterioration in the trade-off between inflation and unemployment does not mean that demand management is no longer effective in reducing inflation, as there is still a correlation between inflation and demand pressures twelve to eighteen months earlier. Second, it should be possible to improve the trade-off significantly — that is, to shift the curve back down and to the left.

The report "ventures a rough guess" that deterioration in the discomfort index up to 1970 was structural, that the 1970-72 improvement was the conventional lagged response of inflation to a downturn in activity, and that the 1972 deterioration was caused by policy mistakes and a clustering of accidents (increases in food, raw-materials and oil prices) that generated stong inflationary expectations. "When demand pressures have increased, inflation has accelerated and vice versa," the group notes. It reads the 1974-76 experience as showing that restrictive demand-management policies are effective against inflation in product markets and rejects the explanation that the slowing of inflation reflects the slowing or reversal of earlier special factors (pp. 106-07). The report goes on to say, however, that "without significant restraint of demand, income would have been expected to start catching up," and this happened in countries "which did not take enough action to restrain demand or make effective use of incomes policy" (p. 107). This statement seems to contradict the idea that demand management will be sufficient to control inflation and suggests that inflation in product markets will lead to pressure to catch up in wages.

The conclusion that the trade-off between inflation and unemployment (or excess capacity) can be improved significantly is based on the hope that experiencing a lower rate of inflation will unwind inflationary expectations. The analysis is expressed in terms of managing demand to restrain inflation and does not deal at all in this section with the problem that expansion may lead to further inflation, rather than to a rise in output and a fall in unemployment. There is no discussion of the employment/output axis of the curve. "Demand management" is referred to throughout as a single instrument, with no differentiation made, in this part of the analysis, between monetary and fiscal policy.

On the question of growth, the report concludes that "reasonably rapid growth remains an appropriate objective" (p. 14). In the next decade, growth will be limited

---

inflation and unemployment have risen at the same time. This has led to a debate as to whether a stable Phillips curve exists in a time of inflationary expectations. The analysis in the report is based on a model in which higher rates of inflation lead to unemployment, not necessarily directly, but because they lead to expectations of restrictive government policy, which in turn discourage investment and production and hence lead ultimately to lower employment (p. 276). The GDP price deflator is used instead of the CPI, and the GDP gap, representing unused potential capacity, is used as a proxy for unemployment in Chart I.

CHART 2

The Narrow Path Back toward Full Employment and Price Stability

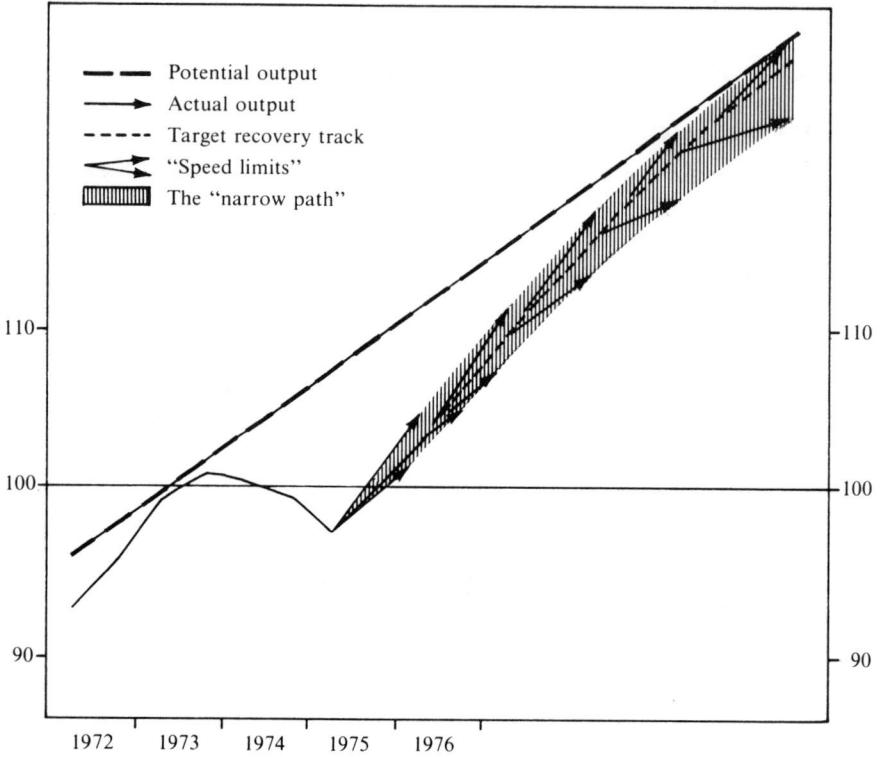

Note: OECD GNP, 1973 = 100; semi-logarithmic scale.
Source: OECD, *op. cit.*, p. 191.

not so much by physical or technological constraints "as by the need to overcome the present economic and social stresses and imbalances, of which inflation is one of the main symptoms" (p. 14). The crucial component of growth is labor productivity, the report maintains, and there is nothing on the supply side to prevent output from growing as rapidly over the next five to ten years as it did in the 1960s.

Policy Recommendations: Toward Full Employment and Price Stability

The Aims of Policy

"The fundamental aim of policy is to return to reasonable rates of growth and high levels of employment" (p. 17). The group prescribes finding "the narrow path" to recovery, as illustrated in Chart 2. The report does not underestimate the difficulties of staying on this narrow path and indicates that getting onto it at all requires the unwinding of inflationary expectations by means of demand management. Since the initial conditions are unfavorable, a moderate expansion is required, during which memories of recent inflation will fade and confidence in rising sales and employment will be restored. An expansion of demand somewhat greater than the growth of potential supply should be sought. The correctly judged track will minimize average unemployment over the recovery period as a whole. It will be difficult, however, to combine rising employment and capacity utilization with a further reduction in the rate of inflation; this will require "skilful and determined use of monetary and fiscal policy, and, where appropriate, prices and incomes policy" (p. 17; see also pp. 182-83). "We reject the view that inflation might offer a way of resolving the underlying conflicts which produced the inflation in the first place" (p. 18).

The report does not indicate how to find the correct track, except by a series of approximations that always slightly undershoot rather than overshoot the target. (The subsequent section on fiscal policy sheds more light on this problem.) Events during 1976, the report notes, confirmed the analysis on which the strategy of a moderate but sustained expansion was based and demonstrated how difficult it will be to achieve such an expansion. "A given increase in demand is more likely to generate inflation and less likely to stimulate investment than would have been the case in the past" (p. 182).

Better Demand-Management Policies

The goal is to steer demand along a narrow path consistent with sustained recovery: the lower limit — sufficient expansion to encourage investment recovery; the upper limit — the point at which a rapid increase in demand would re-ignite inflationary expectations (pp. 189-90).[9] A relatively active, but cautious, policy will be needed. As healthier expectations emerge, monetary and fiscal policy should be framed in the light of medium-term requirements, leaving minor deviations to built-in stabilizers. Steadier and more predictable policies would promote healthy expectations. The recommendations throughout this section are in the direction of refining existing tools of monetary and fiscal management, making their use automatic where possible — that is, subject to rules and guidelines — and reducing purely discretionary action. Success is presumably dependent on the accurate setting of medium-term budgetary targets, a particularly complex task.

Monetary Policy

Public announcement of monetary targets gives concrete expression to government's intention not to accommodate high rates of inflation (p. 193). In the present circumstances the aim should be to reduce these targets progressively over time as inflation is brought down to acceptably low levels. Fluctuations in inflationary expectations translate rather directly into unpredictable changes in nominal interest rates. For this reason, the report finds, monetary authorities should give somewhat more weight to trends in the monetary aggregates and less to interest rates than has generally been the case.

Fiscal Policy

Here it is not a question of doing things differently, but of doing them better. Abandonment of the target of a balanced budget left few guidelines for restraint in

---

[9] Professor Komiya questions the meaning of the "narrow path" concept and the actual consequences of deviating from the limits (p. 250).

public expenditures, and the report is concerned with establishing a firmer framework for fiscal decision-making. "Expenditure and tax policy should be such that over the medium run, at the desired levels of output, employment and prices (and the associated rates of monetary expansion and interest rates), the public sector should run a deficit to match any excess of saving over investment in the private sector (including any savings exported in the form of net capital out-flows), or should run a surplus to offset any deficiency" (p. 199).[10] Deviations that result because the economy is not at desired levels of output and employment — that is, from the operation of automatic stabilizers — should be accepted. Discretionary or conjunctural fiscal action will be needed for stabilization but should either be temporary, be self-liquidating, or take the form of speeding up or slowing down public programs already agreed upon. There is a case for "automating" fiscal policy by legislating trigger mechanisms.

Although selective policies are subject to interest-group pressure, use of temporary fiscal incentives or disincentives to broad categories of demand — business investment, housing, and so forth — has been encouraging, the report finds.

The Interrelationship Between Monetary and Fiscal Policy

Historically, fiscal policy has been used more appropriately than monetary policy. The biggest mistake was the United States' becoming involved in a major war without fully realizing the cost or paying for it. The second and more important lesson about fiscal policy is the danger that short-term demand-management considerations and political pressures may tend to generate a disproportionate growth of the public sector.

The group finds that there is not that close a link between monetary and fiscal policy and that the excessive monetary expansion of the early 1970s was not a function of the need to finance deficits. In the past few years massive deficits have been common, but monetary expansion more moderate. The data suggest that "monetary control is not normally lost in an abnormal recession period and cautious monetary management is not incompatible with appropriate expansionary fiscal action." Deficits have been large because of the severity of the recession and the need "to compensate temporarily for the increase in the world's propensity to save caused by the rise in oil prices and the resulting large external financial surpluses of a few of the major oil-producing countries" (p. 197).

It should be possible, the report finds, to finance budget deficits "without requiring a rate of monetary expansion which would engender inflation later and without raising interest rates so much as to offset the fiscal stimulus through adverse effects on private spending" (p. 197). The danger arises when financial markets and public opinion associate deficits with the likelihood of further inflation. The inflationary expectations of lenders push interest rates upward, forcing the authorities to increase the rate of monetary expansion as an offset. A deficit must be rapidly reduced in the upswing to prevent either inflation or a sharp rise in interest rates together with the crowding out of private borrowing and investment.

---

[10] It may be assumed that the full-employment surplus ought to be zero (at, for example, 4 percent unemployment, as seems to be the common hypothesis in U.S. administrations); but if this is inconsistent with saving desires elsewhere in the economy, such a target can only make the attainment of full employment more difficult, the report notes in an annex (pp. 326-29). A more consistent assumption would recognize the macro-economic equilibrium condition that requires that "government dissaving offset desired household, corporate, and foreign saving." This approach is adopted in the German concept of the cyclically neutral budget.

Appendix

Policies Directly Affecting Employment

When high rates of unemployment can be reduced only gradually for fear of re-igniting inflation, a case can be made for policies — such as additional employment in the public sector — that increase the amount of employment associated with a given increase in aggregate demand. Another possible approach is to give a subsidy to private employers taking on new labor.

Better Reconciliation of Competing Claims

Achievement of growth requires the right combination of conditions concerning composition of demand and distribution of output and incomes. Failure to satisfy these conditions will lead to disequilibrium, which may take the form of underinvestment, unstable balance of payments positions, or a continuation of the combination of inflation and underutilization of capacity experienced over the past few years. As a result, growth will fall short of potential and will eventually impair potential itself. "Ensuring the appropriate structure of demand and avoiding inflation can be framed in terms of the need to reconcile the competing claims on resources exerted by different socio-economic groups." Major claims are those bearing on

- "the need to provide for a satisfactory level of investment, involving in particular the distribution of income between labour and capital;
- the allocation of resources between the public and private sectors;
- the international distribution of output and income between OECD countries and the rest of the world;
- claims arising from competition between consumers for a larger share of the resources available for private consumption" (pp. 155-56).

The Investment Problem

Certain arguments point to the possibility of an investment problem, but the group found the evidence equivocal, and there were differences of opinion as to the seriousness of the problem. The arguments include an accelerated increase in the capital intensity of production in the future; a reduced willingness to invest in productive assets, reflecting reduced profit expectations and uncertainty about growth; and a reduced ability to invest because of lower profits or difficulty in borrowing. The common factor in these arguments is an increase in the cost of key inputs relative to the value of output — principally the cost of energy and environmental protection and the relative real cost of labor. Increases in these costs pose problems for medium-term economic management because they stimulate a shift toward capital-intensive production, requiring that a larger share of output go to investment, and they also reduce profits. If there is normally a stable equilibrium relationship among the relative prices of different basic inputs, recent changes have been far enough from the normal range to cause structural adjustment problems. Therefore, the normal problems of recovery from recession are compounded by an extra dimension.

Wage bargaining reflects a determination to maintain constant, or even increasing, real wage levels, so that the ways in which the competing claims of labor and capital have become resolved are central to the determination of investment.[11]

---

[11] Exchange-rate movements in the 1970s may have depressed investment (for example, in Germany) by effectively increasing real wages. There is, however, an offsetting willingness to increase investment in depreciating countries because of their records of inflation.

With companies unwilling to raise prices, overly rapid increases in the relative real cost of labor create a tendency to higher unemployment, but organized labor may well favor higher real wages at the cost of high unemployment.

In some cases, reduced willingness to invest may be associated with reduced profit expectations (examples are the United States, the United Kingdom, Germany, and Italy). In other countries (Canada, France, and Japan), it is not clear that there has been any significant structural change in the level of profitability (p. 163). If there is a problem, the group concludes, a solution may result only from consensus among government, labor, and management on the need for higher profits.

Public Expenditure

A number of countries went too fast in trying to provide goods and services, which had an adverse effect on their growth and rates of inflation. The rapid automatic growth of public revenues does much to explain this rapid growth of the public sector. Since wage claims are geared to after-tax incomes, increasing public expenditure, matched by higher taxation, can generate "tax-push" inflation. Firmer guidelines as a "speed limit" are a good idea, the report finds, as are arrangements to eliminate fiscal drag.

The report mentions that an earlier OECD study on the factors underlying future demand for public expenditure in various sectors suggested that governments could now slow down the rise in public expenditure if they wished, since health, education, and welfare programs have achieved high coverage. Because there will be continuing pressure for new and expanded programs, however, the public must better understand the costs of increased public service. The report does not suggest that reduction of public expenditure is a panacea for all ills, but it does find that any further shifts of resources to the public sector should be at a rate commensurate with the willingness of the public to bear the cost.

The Foreign Sector

Commitment to achieve an adequate transfer of resources to developing countries is the most important external competing claim on the industrial OECD countries.

Prices and Incomes Policies

The group supports discussions with business and labor, as well as the setting of broad guidelines and applying them in the public sector, but it does not favor intervention on a permanent basis. Devices such as France's "conjunctural levy," which penalizes excess increases in unit wages or profit margins, can, however, narrow the conflict between the public interest and the self-interest of the parties concerned. "It is when we turn to the problems of applying a prices and incomes policy to the private sector that the difficulties — and our doubts — begin to mount up. As we noted earlier, in a highly decentralized economy, with no significant agglomerations of market power, appropriate use of the traditional instruments of demand management could be sufficient to ensure non-inflationary growth" (p. 216).

Better Functioning of Markets

Removal of obstacles to freer play of market forces would be beneficial, the report suggests. It supports traditional labor-market policies designed to reduce

Appendix

mismatches between supply and demand for particular categories of labor and favors increased flexibility in wage structure. Some countries should alter the financing of their social security systems to avoid taxing employment so heavily. Capital markets are generally innovative and competitive, the report finds, and it recommends the removal of institutional obstacles to indexed bonds, which could be issued by governments also. The group favors traditional competition policy in product markets and finds that the most promising route lies in the removal of tariff and non-tariff barriers — especially to manufactured imports from underdeveloped countries. Buffer stocks and more vigorous energy policies are given support.

The International Dimension

Interdependence has made a significant contribution to the difficulties of the past five years. As a result, policy-makers should consult and try to form a view of the need for stimulus or restraint in the world economy as a whole. The report upholds the view that countries with high unemployment, low inflation, a favorable balance of payments, large reserves, and good credit should take the lead in expanding demand (and vice versa for restraint) and maintains that it is a matter of some urgency that a greater share of the oil deficit be borne by credit-worthy countries. It stresses a need for effective domestic anti-inflationary policies in high-inflation countries. "Favourably-placed countries which presently could expand more rapidly without risk of additional inflation should accept responsibility for maintaining the momentum of the recovery in world economic activity"[12] (p. 237; see also p. 184).

Exchange Rates

The group is against a return to pegging and uncertain about the wisdom of intervention. It stresses a need for contingency planning for more active intervention by governments.

International Liquidity

The report expresses concern about the uneven accumulation of debt. There is a need for private lenders to pay more attention to the economic situation in borrowing countries, and for borrowing countries to seek early advice from official institutions. The amount of official financing available to back up stabilization policies and adjustment to higher oil prices should be increased and adequate protection of the system from financial crisis should be provided through arrangements among major central banks.

Assessment

Since the report was undertaken in an international forum, it is disappointing that it takes so little account of the international dimension except to note frequently that it exists. In addition, although the group lays out rather thoroughly the factors that have led to the present predicament, its choice of factors to emphasize and those to downplay results in an under-emphasis on structural change and a heavy empha-

---

[12] Professor Giersch notes that if a country suffers from unemployment and inflation, an expansionary effect imported through reflated demand will rekindle inflation just as in the case of domestic reflation (p. 248). Mr. Komiya argues that "it is misleading to argue for the reduction of divergences in economic performance among OECD countries. It is especially dangerous if the stronger countries are urged to become weaker in order to help the weak" (p. 253).

sis on shocks and on policy errors, which leads to the conviction that traditional tools will solve current problems.

After concluding that deterioration in the Phillips curve can be corrected by demand management, the report goes on to say that as "expectational" inflation subsides, "we may find there has been an acceleration of the inflation that can broadly be attributed to competing claims and malfunctioning of market mechanisms" (p. 108). This statement calls into question the report's assessment that shocks and policy errors were more important than structural problems in the first place. In the same way, by underplaying the problems of stimulating investment, the report neglects the supply and output side of the economic equation, concentrating heavily on demand. Lack of consensus on the importance of the investment problem represented the principal area of disagreement within the group.

The report breaks little new ground and concentrates on the desirability of making existing tools more automatic, so that policy is less susceptible to human error. While all this may well be a move in the right direction, it hardly seems an adequate solution to the whole range of problems facing industrial economies today. The group admits that the economic starting point is bad and the path difficult, but it does not adequately explore the possibility that demand management may not result in an improved trade-off between "activity" and inflation in the longer term.

Members of the Group

Paul McCracken, Chairman	Professor at the University of Michigan and former Chairman of the United States Council of Economic Advisers
Guido Carli	President, Confindustria, and former Governor of the Bank of Italy
Herbert Giersch	Director of the Institute of World Economics at Kiel University and former Member of the German Council of Economic Advisers
Attila Karaosmanoglu	Director of Development Policy at the IBRD and former Deputy Prime Minister for Economic Affairs in the Turkish government
Ryutaro Komiya	Professor at the University of Tokyo
Assar Lindbeck	Director of the Institute for International Economic Studies at Stockholm University
Robert Marjolin*	Former Secretary-General of OEEC and Vice-President of the Commission of the European Economic Community
Robin Matthews	Master of Clare College, Cambridge, and former Drummond Professor of Political Economy, Oxford University

*Robert Marjolin replaced Raymond Barre upon his entry into the French government.

Footnotes to the Statement

Sir Richard Dobson: Having read Mr. Beigie's paper on inflation, which on the whole I find entirely admirable, there is one statement with which I must take issue.

In Chapter 4, "Structural Problems and Their Impacts," I find the following statement: "Capital 'shortages' always exist, in the sense that more investment can be placed at positive real rates of return than funds are available to finance."

I find this statement inconsistent not only with some of the other comments earlier in the same chapter (for example, "the threat of price or profit controls inhibits any necessary rise in the rate of return on capital from occurring") but also with my own observations in an inflationary era.

Certainly as far as Britain is concerned — and I suspect the same applies to North America — individual or institutional investors in the stock exchanges in the past four or five years have seen not only the real value of their investments but also the purchasing power of their dividends declining. Comparatively few companies are richer in real terms over this period, and not very many in the United Kingdom would have wished to increase their dividends much above 10 percent per annum even if they had had the choice.

Mr. Beigie points out that government demands on capital clearly eat into the existing capital stock, reducing the free capital available for entrepreneurial investments. At the same time, nationalisation has reduced the scope for the investment of the residue. In the United Kingdom the private investor is largely precluded from putting his money into what were once growth activities — steel, shipbuilding, motor manufacture, and utilities, for example.

Investment in government or other fixed interest securities may produce "positive real" rates of return in the short term but are seldom sufficient to cover the loss of purchasing power of the investment in the longer term.

I have been referring to returns on investment before taxation of the investor. The normal tax rates in force in our three countries — not to mention the punitive rates on investment income in the United Kingdom — at present entirely prevent the private investor from maintaining the real value of his capital, even if he reinvests every penny of net after-tax yield.

Apart from individuals, I know of many major companies and institutions on both sides of the Atlantic that have at their disposal very substantial sums of cash which they would gladly invest in creative enterprises if, without excessive risk, they could be confident of maintaining the purchasing power of these funds even without the expectation of any "real return" in an incremental sense.

Sir Richard Powell: The case against income controls, statutory or voluntary, seems to me a good deal stronger than Mr. Beigie suggests in the section on the subject in Chapter VI. U.K. experience has been that periods of control normally end sooner or later in a wage and salary explosion, after which the general level of incomes is no lower than if there had been no control; and the rigidities and distortions that invariably accompany control have had wholly destructive consequences in removing flexibility; preventing differentiation between sectors of the economy and individual companies according to economic circumstances and ability to pay; weakening incentive; and narrowing differentials to allow for skill and responsibility. Income control may perhaps have a place in the system if it takes the form of a short freeze as part of a "crunch" operation; but any satisfactory long-term or permanent control seems entirely impracticable in a highly complex, advanced industrial economy, as well as being injurious to social and economic well-being.

Jacob Sheinkman: While I am in agreement with the major thrust of this statement, I wish to note my exceptions to the policy biases of the report's recommendations. As Carl Beigie himself notes, gradualism in pursuit of discipline does not seem to be working. I am not convinced that the refinements he urges would improve the track record.

The labor movement in the United States has addressed itself primarily to the inflationary impacts of structural rigidities, such as those reflected in the costs of food, energy, housing and medical care, as well as in the pricing strategies of large corporations. In these areas, restraints on the money supply and resulting higher interest rates have generally served to fuel further price advances. Similarly, tax programs should be structured to serve growth objectives as well as fiscal-policy objectives. Thus any incentives to business financed through the tax system should be targeted toward specific objectives, such as expanded research and development outlays, rather than across-the-board tax relief to corporations.

In my view, economic growth is the key to both jobs and inflation. In this respect, the report hedges unnecessarily in suggesting that, in the United States, stimulus to prevent a rise in the unemployment rate may not be appropriate now and that the unemployment rate constituting full employment there may be closer to 6 percent than 4 percent. As Alice Rivlin of the Congressional Budget Office has noted, if measures to reduce structural imbalances in the labor market were adopted and effective, a non-inflationary employment rate in the United States could potentially be even lower than 3 percent.

Members of the British-North American Committee

Chairmen
SIR RICHARD DOBSON
President, B.A.T. Industries Limited,
London

IAN MacGREGOR
General Partner, Lazard Frères & Co.,
New York, Honorary Chairman,
AMAX Inc., Greenwich, Connecticut

Vice Chairmen
SIR ALASTAIR DOWN
Chairman, Burmah Oil Company,
Swindon

GEORGE P. SHULTZ
President, Bechtel Corporation,
San Francisco, California

Chairman, Executive Committee
WILLIAM I. M. TURNER, JR.
President and Chief Executive Officer,
Consolidated-Bathurst Inc.,
Montreal, Quebec

Members
WILLIAM S. ANDERSON
Chairman of the Board,
NCR Corporation, Dayton, Ohio

J. A. ARMSTRONG
Chairman and Chief Executive Officer,
Imperial Oil Limited, Toronto, Ontario

*JOSEPH E. BAIRD
President and Chief Operating Officer,
Occidental Petroleum Corporation,
Los Angeles, California

A. E. BALLOCH
Executive Vice President, Bowater
Incorporated, Old Greenwich, Connecticut

ROBERT A. BANDEEN
President and Chief Executive Officer,
Canadian National, Montreal, Quebec

SIR DONALD BARRON
Group Chairman, Rowntree Mackintosh
Limited, York

DAVID BASNETT
General Secretary, General & Municipal
Workers' Union, Esher, Surrey

CARL E. BEIGIE
President and Chief Executive Officer,
C. D. Howe Research Institute,
Montreal, Quebec

ROBERT BELGRAVE
Policy Adviser, British Petroleum Ltd.,
London

I. H. STUART BLACK
Chairman, General Accident Fire and
Life Assurance Corporation Ltd.,
Perth, Scotland

JOHN F. BOOKOUT
President and Chief Executive Officer,
Shell Oil Company, Houston, Texas

*T. F. BRADSHAW
President, Atlantic Richfield Company,
Los Angeles, California

JOHN F. BURLINGAME
Vice President and Group Executive,
International and Canadian Group,
General Electric Company,
Fairfield, Connecticut

SIR CHARLES CARTER
Chairman of Research and Management
Committee, Policy Studies Institute,
London

J. EDWIN CARTER
Chairman and Chief Executive Officer,
INCO Limited, Toronto, Ontario

SILAS S. CATHCART
Chairman & Chief Executive Officer,
Illinois Tool Works, Inc.,
Chicago, Illinois

SIR FREDERICK CATHERWOOD
Chairman, British Overseas Trade Board,
London

HAROLD van B. CLEVELAND
Vice President, Citibank, New York,
New York

JAN COLLINS
Chairman, William Collins & Sons,
Glasgow, Scotland

---

*Became a member of the Committee after statement was circulated for signature.

KIT COPE
Overseas Director, Confederation of
British Industry, London

DONALD M. COX
Director and Senior Vice President,
Exxon Corporation, New York, New York

RALPH J. CRAWFORD, JR.
Vice Chairman of the Board, Wells Fargo
Bank, San Francisco, California

FRANK J. CUMMISKEY
IBM Vice President and President,
General Business Group/International,
IBM Corporation, White Plains,
New York

JAMES W. DAVANT
Chairman of the Board and Chief
Executive Officer, Paine, Webber, Jackson
& Curtis Inc., New York, New York

DIRK DE BRUYNE
Managing Director, Royal Dutch/Shell
Group of Companies, London

MICHAEL D. DINGMAN
President & Chief Executive Officer,
Wheelabrator-Frye Inc., Hampton,
New Hampshire

WILLIAM DODGE
Ottawa, Ontario

GEOFFREY DRAIN
General Secretary, National Association
of Local Government Officers, London

JOHN DU CANE
Chairman and Managing Director,
Selection Trust Ltd., London

DONALD V. EARNSHAW
Senior Staff Executive, Continental Can
Company, Stamford, Connecticut

GERRY EASTWOOD
General Secretary, Association of
Patternmakers and Allied Craftsmen,
London

HARRY E. EKBLOM
Chairman and Chief Executive Officer,
European American Bancorp, New York,
New York

MOSS EVANS
General Secretary, Transport & General
Workers' Union, London

J. K. FINLAYSON
Vice Chairman, The Royal Bank of
Canada, Montreal, Quebec

GLENN FLATEN
First Vice President, Canadian Federation
of Agriculture, Regina, Saskatchewan

ROBERT M. FOWLER
Chairman, Executive Committee,
C. D. Howe Research Institute,
Montreal, Quebec

GWAIN H. GILLESPIE
Senior Vice President — Finance,
Heublein Inc., Farmington, Connecticut

MALCOLM GLENN
Executive Vice President, Reed Holdings
Inc., Reed International, Ltd., London

GEORGE GOYDER
British Secretary, British-North American
Committee, London

HON. HENRY HANKEY
Director, Lloyds Bank International Ltd.,
London

AUGUSTIN S. HART, JR.
Vice Chairman, Quaker Oats Company,
Chicago, Illinois

G. R. HEFFERNAN
President, Co-Steel International Ltd.,
Whitby, Ontario

HENRY J. HEINZ II
Chairman of the Board, H. J. Heinz
Company, Pittsburgh, Pennsylvania

ROBERT HENDERSON
Chairman, Kleinwort Benson Ltd.,
London

ROBERT P. HENDERSON
President and Chief Executive Officer,
Itek Corporation, Lexington,
Massachusetts

JACK HENDLEY
General Manager (International),
Midland Bank Ltd., London

Committee Members

HENDRIK S. HOUTHAKKER
Professor of Economics, Harvard
University, Cambridge, Massachusetts

TOM JACKSON
General Secretary, Union of Post Office
Workers, Clapham, London

DEAN DONALD P. JACOBS
Graduate School of Management,
Northwestern University, Evanston,
Illinois

JOHN V. JAMES
Chairman of the Board, President, and
Chief Executive Officer, Dresser
Industries, Inc., Dallas, Texas

GEORGE S. JOHNSTON
President, Scudder, Stevens & Clark,
New York, New York

JOSEPH D. KEENAN
President, Union Label and Service
Trades Department, AFL-CIO,
Washington, D.C.

TOM KILLEFER
President, United States Trust Company
of New York, New York, New York

CURTIS M. KLAERNER
Executive Vice President and Director,
Mobil Oil Corporation, New York,
New York

H. U. A. LAMBERT
Chairman, Barclays Bank International
Limited, London

HERBERT H. LANK
Hon. Director, Du Pont of Canada Ltd.,
Montreal, Quebec

WILLIAM A. LIFFERS
Vice Chairman, American Cyanamid
Company, Wayne, New Jersey

JAY LOVESTONE
International Affairs Consultant,
AFL-CIO, Washington, D.C.

RAY W. MACDONALD
Honorary Chairman, Burroughs
Corporation, Grosse Pointe, Michigan

CARGILL MacMILLAN, JR.
Senior Vice President, Cargill Inc.,
Minneapolis, Minnesota

J. P. MANN
Deputy Chairman, United Biscuits
Holdings Ltd., Middlesex

A. B. MARSHALL
Managing Director, P & O Steam
Navigation Company, London

DENNIS McDERMOTT
President, Canadian Labour Congress,
Ottawa, Ontario

WILLIAM J. McDONOUGH
Executive Vice President, International
Banking Department, The First National
Bank of Chicago, Chicago, Illinois

WILLIAM C. Y. McGREGOR
International Vice President, Brotherhood
of Railway, Airline & Steamship Clerks,
Montreal, Quebec

DONALD E. MEADS
Chairman and President, Carver
Associates, Plymouth Meeting,
Pennsylvania

PATRICK MEANEY
Group Managing Director, Thomas
Tilling Limited, London

C. J. MEDBERRY, III
Chairman of the Board, BankAmerica
Corporation & Bank of America NT & SA,
Los Angeles, California

SIR PETER MENZIES
Welwyn, Herts

JOHN MILLER
President, National Planning Association,
Washington, D.C.

DEREK F. MITCHELL
Chairman & Chief Executive Officer,
BP Canada Limited, Montreal, Quebec

JOSEPH P. MONGE
Rancho Santa Fe, California

DONALD R. MONTGOMERY
Secretary-Treasurer, Canadian Labour
Congress, Ottawa, Ontario

MALCOLM MOOS
Hackensack, Minnesota

KENNETH D. NADEN
President, National Council of Farm Cooperatives, Washington, D.C.

WILLIAM L. NAUMANN
Former Chairman of the Board, Caterpillar Tractor Company, Peoria, Illinois

WILLIAM S. OGDEN
Executive Vice President, The Chase Manhattan Bank, N.A., New York, New York

PAUL PARÉ
President and Chief Executive Officer, Imasco Ltd., Montreal, Quebec

BROUGHTON PIPKIN
Chairman, BICC Limited, London

SIR RICHARD POWELL
Director, Hill Samuel Group Ltd., London

J. G. PRENTICE
Chairman of the Board, Canadian Forest Products, Ltd., Vancouver, British Columbia

LOUIS PUTZE
Director and Consultant, Rockwell International, Pittsburgh, Pennsylvania

BEN ROBERTS
Professor of Industrial Relations, London School of Economics, London

HAROLD B. ROSE
Group Economic Adviser, Barclays Bank Limited, London

DAVID SAINSBURY
Director of Finance, J. Sainsbury Ltd., London

WILLIAM SALOMON
Managing Partner, Salomon Brothers, New York, New York

A. C. I. SAMUEL
Director General, International Group of the National Association of Pesticide Manufacturers, London

NATHANIEL SAMUELS
Vice Chairman, Kuhn Loeb Lehman Brothers International, Chairman, Louis Dreyfus Holding Company, Inc., New York, New York

SIR FRANCIS SANDILANDS
Chairman, Commercial Union Assurance Company, Limited, London

HON. MAURICE SAUVÉ
Executive Vice President, Administrative and Public Affairs, Consolidated-Bathurst Inc., Montreal, Quebec

PETER F. SCOTT
Chairman, Provincial Insurance Company, Ltd., Kendal, Westmoreland

ROBERT C. SEAMANS, JR.
Massachusetts Institute of Technology, Cambridge, Massachusetts

LORD SEEBOHM
Chairman, Finance for Industry, London

THE EARL OF SELKIRK
President, Royal Central Asian Society, London

JACOB SHEINKMAN
General Secretary-Treasurer, Amalgamated Clothing and Textile Workers' Union, New York, New York

LORD SHERFIELD
Chairman, Raytheon Europe International Company, London

R. MICHAEL SHIELDS
Managing Director, Associated Newspapers Group Ltd., London

GEORGE L. SHINN
Chairman, The First Boston Corporation, New York, New York

WILLIAM E. SIMON
New York, New York

LAUREN K. SOTH
West Des Moines, Iowa

E. NORMAN STAUB
Chairman and Chief Executive Officer, The Northern Trust Company, Chicago, Illinois

RALPH I. STRAUS
New York, New York

JAMES A. SUMMER
Excelsior, Minnesota

Committee Members

HAROLD SWEATT
Honorary Chairman of the Board,
Honeywell, Inc., Minneapolis, Minnesota

SIR ROBERT TAYLOR
Deputy Chairman, Standard Chartered
Bank Ltd., London

A. A. THORNBROUGH
Deputy Chairman and Chief Executive
Officer, Massey-Ferguson Limited,
Toronto, Ontario

SIR MARK TURNER
Chairman, Rio Tinto-Zinc Corporation
Ltd., London

JOHN W. TUTHILL
President, The Salzburg Seminar,
Cambridge, Massachusetts

W. O. TWAITS
Toronto, Ontario

MARTHA R. WALLACE
Executive Director and Director,
The Henry Luce Foundation, Inc.,
New York, New York

RICHARD C. WARREN
Consultant, IBM Corporation, Armonk,
New York

GLENN E. WATTS
President, Communications Workers of
America, AFL-CIO, Washington, D.C.

W. L. WEARLY
Chairman, Ingersoll-Rand Company,
Woodcliff Lake, New Jersey

VISCOUNT WEIR
Chairman and Chief Executive, The Weir
Group Limited, Glasgow, Scotland

HUNTER P. WHARTON
General President Emeritus, International
Union of Operating Engineers,
Washington, D.C.

WILLIAM W. WINPISINGER
President, International Association of
Machinists and Aerospace Workers,
Washington, D.C.

SIR ERNEST WOODROOFE
Former Chairman, Unilever Ltd.,
Guildford, Surrey

Inactive Status
C. FRED BERGSTEN

Sponsoring Organizations

The British-North American Research Association was inaugurated in December, 1969, as an independent, non-profit-making organization. Its primary purpose is to sponsor research on British-North American economic relations in association with the British-North American Committee. Publications of the British-North American Research Association as well as those of the British-North American Committee are available at the Association's office, 1 Gough Square, London EC4A 3DE (Tel. 01-353-6371).

The Association is a registered educational charity and is governed by a council under the chairmanship of Sir Richard Dobson.

The National Planning Association is an independent, private, non-profit, non-political organization that carries on research and policy formulation in the public interest. NPA was founded during the Great Depression of the 1930s, when conflicts among the major economic groups — business, farmers, and labor — threatened to paralyze national decision-making on the critical issues confronting American society. It was dedicated, in the words of its statement of purpose, to the task "of getting [these] diverse groups to work together . . . [and] to provide on specific problems concrete programs for action planned in the best traditions of a functioning democracy." Such democratic planning, NPA believes, involves the development of effective governmental and private policies and programs not only by official agencies but also through the independent initiative and cooperation of the main private-sector groups concerned. To preserve and strengthen American political and economic democracy, therefore, the necessary government actions have to be consistent with, and supportive of, a dynamic private sector.

NPA brings together influential and knowledgeable leaders from business, labor, agriculture, and the applied and academic professions to serve on policy committees, one of which is the British-North American Committee. These committees identify emerging problems confronting the nation at home and abroad and seek to develop and agree upon policies and programs for coping with them. The research and writing for these committees are provided by NPA's professional staff and, as required, by outside experts.

In addition, NPA's professional staff undertakes research designed to provide data and ideas for policy-makers and -planners in government and the private sector. This research includes the preparation on a regular basis of economic and demographic projections for the national economy, regions, states, and metropolitan areas; the development of program planning and evaluation techniques; research on national goals and priorities; analyses of welfare and dependency problems, employment and manpower needs, education, medical care, environmental protection, energy, and other economic and social is-

Sponsoring Organizations 81

sues confronting American society; and studies of changing international realities and their implications for U.S. policies.

NPA publications, including those of the British-North American Committee, can be obtained from the Association's offices, 1606 New Hampshire Avenue, N.W., Washington, D.C. 20009 (Tel. 202-265-7685).

The C. D. Howe Research Institute is a private, non-political, non-profit organization founded in January, 1973, by the merger of the C. D. Howe Memorial Foundation and the Private Planning Association of Canada, to undertake research into Canadian economic policy issues, with emphasis on fiscal, monetary, and international trade policy.

HRI continues the activities of the PPAC. These include the work of three established committees, composed of agricultural, business, educational, labor, and professional leaders. The committees are the Canadian Economic Policy Committee, which since 1961 has been concentrating on Canadian economic issues; the Canadian-American Committee, which has dealt with relations between Canada and the United States since 1957 and is jointly sponsored by the National Planning Association in Washington and HRI; and the British-North American Committee, formed in 1969 and sponsored jointly by the British-North American Research Association in London, the National Planning Association, and HRI. Each of the three committees meets twice a year to consider important current issues and to sponsor and review studies that contribute to a better public understanding of such issues.

In addition to taking over the publications of the three PPAC committees, HRI releases the work of its staff, and occasionally of outside authors, in four other publications: *HRI Observations*, a number of which are published each year; *Policy Review and Outlook*, published annually; *Special Studies*, to provide detailed analysis of major policy issues; and *Commentaries*, to give wide circulation to the views of experts on issues of current Canadian interest.

HRI publications, including those of the British-North American Committee, are available from the Institute's offices, 2064 Sun Life Building, Montreal, Quebec H3B 2X7 (Tel. 514-879-1254).